MW00988755

Published from
Mardukite Borsippa HQ, San Luis Valley, Colorado

Mardukite Research Library Catalogue No. "Liber-R9" (R+9)

Graphics assistance by Kyra Kaos

10TH ANNIVERSARY – COLLECTOR'S EDITION

NOVEM PORTIS

NECRONOMICON REVELATIONS AND NINE GATES OF THE KINGDOM OF SHADOWS

written by Joshua Free
with Foreword by Rowen Gardner

First published in 2011 combining two volumes:
"Necronomicon Revelations" and "Liber-9"

JOSHUA FREE
publishing imprint

© 2021, JOSHUA FREE

ISBN : 978-0-578-84334-6

cum superiorum privilegio veniaque

10th Anniversary Collector's Edition—February 2021

—TABLET OF CONTENTS—

THE 10TH ANNIVERSARY INTRODUCTION TO THE "NOVEM PORTIS" COLLECTOR'S EDITION

a foreword by Rowen Gardner

This original classic underground bestseller by Joshua Free returns to print, commemorating its 10th Anniversary with a special hardcover collector's edition that is sure to become a prized addition to your personal esoteric library.

A refreshingly coherent revelation for our times, illuminating long-lost remnants of primordial spirituality, ancient Mesopotamian religion, Sumerian Anunnaki mythology and a hidden mystery tradition developed during a nearly-prehistoric Babylonian era of magic and Otherworldly encounters.

From original Anunnaki traditions to the origins of all worldly and metaphysical systems; from the Yezidic and Persian lore of the Ancient Near East to the past century of underground occult traditions inspired by Aleister Crowley and Kenneth Grant; from the archetypal themes present in the *"Delomelanicon"* to the experiences of the millions of people who have read, or even *used*, Simon's *Necronomicon*... No cuneiform tablet is left unturned, no dark corner left undiscovered, in this amazing and concise guide to the forbidden knowledge lost thousands of years ago, and yet now covertly infused within the heart of all "magick," "religion" and "spirituality" on the planet today.

In *"Novem Portis: Necronomicon Revelations and Nine Gates of the Kingdom of Shadows,"* world renown director of the "Mardukite Research Organization" and founder of "Mardukite Zuism" and the Systemology Society, invites the Seeker on an incredible and practical occult journey into underground esoterica, unlike anything ever published before.

Joshua Free candidly reveals how "spiritual beings" and "alien intelligences" have increasingly influenced the imaginations of "metaphysical" writers and "fantasy" artists, primordial "gods" seeking to have their stories told and knowledge of their existence reborn.

And what's more: the power and influence of this *invisible hand* appear to be behind *all* of the primary systems installed into human civilization, whether social or mystical, since the time of the ancient Sumerians.

This collector's edition hardcover 10th anniversary edition of *"Novem Portis"* combines materials from the revolutionary and controversial *"Necronomicon Revelations"* (*Liber-R*) with the Mardukite Tablet Catalogue released in "Liber-9," just as it appeared a decade ago for the first wave of graduating "Mardukite Chamberlains" alumni, those having previously dedicated two years to a tradition of literary work and spiritual systemology inspired by Joshua Free's *"Necronomicon: The Anunnaki Bible."*

◊ ◊ ◊   ◊ ◊ ◊   ◊ ◊ ◊

Between 2008 and 2018, a team of networked individuals from all over the planet worked diligently as the "Mardukite Chamberlains" (or "Mardukite Research Organization")—along with its "Council of Nabu-Tutu" (operating as a global epicenter of "Mardukite Ministries" and "Mardukite Zuism")—to produce an internal esoteric library that met the standards of our own purposes. Much of this was published underground by "Mardukite Truth Seeker Press" until 2018, when all reprint rights for the literary legacy passed to a new independent press operated by its founder: the "Joshua Free Imprint."

With passage of over a decade, this unique "Mardukite" genre or paradigm is now completely catalogued: spanning everything from prehistoric cosmogenesis of universal origins, through the evolution of the Human Condition and its social development as "traditions" among civic and indigenous populations alike. But more than simply a chronological record of history, the work of Joshua Free provides a Seeker with a progressive understanding of esoteric and spiritual technologies present in this Universe—and practical knowledge, at each stage of the Pathway, that may be directly applied to improve our lives.

"Novem Portis" reflects two critical "completion points" in the original development of the Mardukite Core—*"Liber-9,"* released at the end of 2009 to finalize the original Year-1 cycle of materials for what is now known as *"Necronomicon: The Anunnaki Bible"*; and then *"Liber-R,"* better known as *"Necronomicon Revelations,"* which completed the Mardukite Chamberlains Year-2 cycle at the end of 2010. The entire "Mardukite Core" is now available in a single hardcover Master Edition anthology, titled: *"Necronomicon: The Complete Anunnaki Legacy."*

The two works—*Liber-9* and *Liber-R*—were related in more ways than simply "ends" of a cycle. In fact, the following year, in early 2011, a limited edition paperback printing appeared for a short time, which combined them as *"Novem Portis: Necronomicon Revelations and Nine Gates of the Kingdom of Shadows"*—exactly like the book you now hold in your hands, released for the first time in hardcover to commemorate its 10th Anniversary.

Of course, a reader will soon discover the facets of this presentation are both valid and ironic simultaneously. Joshua Free's *"Nine Gates"* material has always been popular in the "occult underground," but not necessarily for its intended purposes.

Released a year apart from one another—and each completing their own cycle of research—Joshua Free now makes no secret, when instructing the Mardukite Academy of Systemology, that both *libros* were attempts at bridging the end of what is now considered a "Grade-II" treatment of the Mesopotamian Mystery Tradition with the higher levels of understanding and realizations reflecting Mardukite Systemology, which now is to say "Grade-III."

The "Grades" are a new addition to the Legacy. In 2019, the Mardukite Academy established a systematic arrangement of *all* works released by Joshua Free in the past twenty-five years. Then, in late 2020, he instructed the now legendary "Mardukite Master Course" to ensure that a master-level understanding of the first three Grades reached the public via certified "Instructors" and "Masters" of the material. These 48 lectures have since been released on Audio-CD format from the Mardukite Academy —and a complete volume of transcripts is scheduled for release from the "Joshua Free Imprint" in mid-2021.

The basic sentiment relayed at an Academy level has allowed me to come to the conclusion that "Bridging to Systemology" was always the end-goal of the Mardukite Chamberlains. Of course, only materials for "Liber-9" were suited for the "Mardukite Tablet Catalogue" that appears in *"Necronomicon: Anunnaki Bible,"* but the intention was always to use such a platform or foundation or "Bible" to *reach even higher*—and not necessarily get lost in cementing the patterns of past cultures or fragmented beliefs.

Thus, *"Liber-R"* continued exactly where *"Liber-9"* left off, since a year later, even after the completion of a second cycle of work —including *"Sumerian Religion"* and *"Book of Marduk by Nabu"* and *"Babylonian Magic"*—the Mardukite Research Organization was not yet much closer to solidly delivering "Systemology" as a workable "advanced spiritual technology" in 2010.

Although Joshua Free's essay (included herein) titled "Nine Gates of the Kingdom of Shadows" served as the introduction to both *"Liber-9"* and *"Liber-R,"* there were few beyond the small circle of "Mardukite Alumni" that understood underlying "systemological" significances suggested by this: we were working toward a *Pathway* that actually reached *beyond* all of this.

For many of the individuals—Mardukite Seekers—that followed along with these developments in "real-time," it was during the Year-2 cycle of work in 2010, that much of what concealed itself within Year-1 work—and even its prior developments—began to come into focus more clearly, even among those that had been closely involved the whole time. For many of us, these new apexes of realization and understanding were reached during the work found within this edition of *"Novem Portis."*

It seems logical now, after the fact, that the Mardukite Chamberlains spent a year in 2010 working off of supplements to our new "Bible," when certainly *"Necronomicon: The Anunnaki Bible"* was *just that*, a "Bible"—a collected works anthology of ancient renderings that still required some additional background if we were going to establish a solid platform to work from; which has now evolved into "Mardukite Zuism" and its "Systemology."

"*Novem Portis*" material represented a pivotal point in the ongoing developments "behind-the-scenes" at the Mardukite Org. Although it took nearly another decade for the work from "*Systemology: The Original Thesis*" to publicly evolve, it was after the "Liber-R" released in late 2010—and its reissue with "Liber-9" as "*Novem Portis*" in early 2011—that Joshua Free proceeded to dedicate the next ten years of personal life to uncovering "higher grade" "upper route" work, published as Mardukite "Grade-III" texts in 2019: "*The Tablets of Destiny*" and "*Crystal Clear.*"

The material within the book you now hold actually requires very little introduction. It will be undoubtedly read and understood differently for each individual—and its meaning will take on greater shape and form as a Seeker explores the other elements or facets of the esoteric library that it is an integral part of. No two reading of this material seem to yield the same result. The significance evolves synchronous with the Seeker.

It is my hope, following in line with the author's original intentions, that a Seeker will use the stable ledge provided within the Mardukite Core and permit themselves the freedom to *reach higher* into the new vistas now available within the intellectual and spiritual domains of "Mardukite Zuism" and "Systemology."

Wishing you the best, from the arms of the Dragon.

—Rowen Gardner
New Year's Day, 2021
Wales, U.K.

NOVEM PORTIS

THE ANUNNAKI LEGACY
& MAGICAL REVIVAL

Arrival of the "Simon *Necronomicon*" in the mid-1970's did little to satisfy dedicated "Lovecraftian" fanatics—those searching for the legendary book alluded to in a specific series of stories known as the "*Cthulhu Mythos.*" *Howard Phillips (H.P.) Lovecraft's* gothic fantasies elusively described a primordial pantheon of "Ancient Ones" and a legacy they left behind in literary form— the "*Necronomicon*"—many of his readers believed the book had to be *real*, and that the mythos he suggested must somehow exist at the heart of *real* prehistory. Using a platform of fiction, and sparking a new literary genre, H.P. Lovecraft *did* imagine his stories into being, but they were not based on any research or historical fascination—they were the product of astral torment and nightmares.

In 1904, famed occultist *Aleister Crowley* was compelled to spend the spring equinox—the ancient Babylonian "Akitu" New Year— in Egypt. There, he encountered a member of the *Anunnaki*, which explained to him that the "Equinox of the Gods" was taking place—"the *gate* forced open" into a "new aeon." Crowley had traversed the "*Nabu Gate*," making contact with an entity best identified as "*Thoth*"—but who is, in fact, another face of *Nabu*, divine-scribe and son of *Marduk*—a master of the esoteric arts of magic and science. The Hermetic Order of the Golden Dawn had successfully tapped the "*Moon Gate*" previously, as did many other groups and practitioners of the "magical revival." Politics that led to fracturing an alliance between *Crowley* and the *Golden Dawn* concerned "control" of the "*Nabu Gate*"—the *Gate of Thoth, Hermes and Mercury*, among other names.

To the surface world (even the contemporary "New Age") this is all unofficial, of course. All initiates have their own semantics to describe these events. However, the result of Crowley's personal efforts (used to base his own tradition)—"*Book of the Law*"—is just one of many *Anunnaki* transmissions granted to receptive mystics on the planet during the modern magical revival:—

"Every man and woman is a star."

Although popularized later by Kenneth Grant for the O.T.O., Aleister Crowley never once used the word: *Necronomicon*. Based on popular ceremonial magic of the era, his arsenal of medieval and kabbalistic grimoires already possessed their own titles, ones well-recognized today in the "New Age" community. His favorites were the "*Book of Abramelin*," the "*Greater Key of Solomon*" and its "*Goetia*." Crowley even assisted Gerald Gardner in developing the original "*Book of Shadows*," thus directly influencing the large religious movement that sprang from it: *Wicca*.

Of the available grimoires, consensus among early members of the *Mardukite Research Organization* (in 2009) demonstrated that the "divine magic" style reflected from Abramelin-the-Mage, was the preferred example for our own work. It carries a higher "mystical value" than the other "magical" volumes available that may partly resemble the type of ritualistic work thought to be connected to the "*Necronomicon* of H.P. Lovecraft"—of which we are only left with brief passages amidst his stories. The very idea that the "gate-work" itself will "kill" is ridiculously false, as Aleister Crowley lives on for another four decades after the Egypt-incident.

H.P. Lovecraft was only 14 years old in 1904. It was, however, the year that ultimately changed his life. The death of his grandfather left the family in ruin—they were still trying to overcome the loss of his father in 1898. Four years later, when Lovecraft suffered a "nervous breakdown," he was unable to complete his high-school education. It becomes clear that the visions he beheld—resulting in volumes of poetry and short stories—did not come from any logical source: an occult education, bizarre interests, or even mystical mythologies, but were, instead, the product of living beneath the shadows of despair, enduring a perpetual "dark night of the soul" that would never lift at dawn.

Some scholars have gone to great lengths to prove that Lovecraft's grandfather was a very active Freemason, but there does not seem to be any direct "spill-over" interest for either Lovecraft or his father. The only work of mythology (we know for certain) that appealed to Lovecraft and may have any relevance to his later work, is "*Arabian Nights.*" And before using the Greek name "*Necronomicon,*" Lovecraft proposes that the legendary work first bore the Arabic title "*Al Azif.*" Descriptions of Lovecraft's "*Al-Alif*" also share some similarities to the Yezidi "*Al-Jilwah,*"—given as Mardukite *Tablet-J* (from "*Liber-9,*" included in this anthology). It would seem to some that Lovecraft did manage to access the *Gates* directly—or, like Crowley, was *directed to them intentionally.*

The cosmic "dualism" present in Lovecraft's work is out of synch with the original Sumerian Anunnaki pantheon or tradition. Themes of "dualism" really develop more strongly in later Semitic and Zoroastrian interpretations of the *Anunnaki* system—and also from Egypt. For this reason, many skeptics attacked the "Mesopotamian mysticism" presented in the Simon *Necronomicon*—but, if there is some validity behind all of this, then it alludes to something that was not even known to *Sumerians* concerning origins of their gods—something that would become emphasized later by *Babylonians.*

Lovecraftian stories describe the malignant force of "*Ancient Ones*" that at one time reign supreme in the cosmos but are later defeated by a younger generation of "*Elder Gods*"—those responsible for the creation of men and the inhabitable ("civilized") earth. There is no evidence for this in Sumer, and the closest resembling cycle from the *Ancient Near East* that could apply is none other than the "Mardukite" Babylonian paradigm—centralized on the "*Enuma Eliš.*

If we are to consider one possible connection ancient lore where Lovecraft could possibly pull his "Cthulhu mythos" from, it is the mythology painted of TIAMAT in the *Enuma Eliš*—rendered as *Tablet-N* and *Tablet-F* from Mardukite *"Necronomicon: The Anunnaki Bible"*—a Babylonian worldview, *not* Sumerian. It resembles the discordance among primordial gods that Lovecraft alludes to more closely than anything else.

Consider (*Necronomicon: The Anunnaki Bible*):—

"When first the gods were [like] men on Earth."

Compared to (*Necronomicon of H.P. Lovecraft*):—

"The spawn of the Old Ones covered the Earth
and their children endure throughout the Ages."

Lovecraft continues (from the Hay *Necronomicon*):—

"And the Elder Gods opened their eyes
and beheld abominations..."

The bizarre horrors described in "H.P. Lovecraft's *Necronomicon*" appear in the *"Enuma Eliš"* concerning a primordial battle between the "Ancient Ones" [TIAMAT and ABZU] and the "Elder Gods" [the *Anunnaki*]. Much as the "younger gods" displaced their forefathers in post-Sumerian traditions, we can see this was probably the case here. TIAMAT and ABZU are not necessarily a "malignant" force, but in the Babylonian "Epic of Creation" (the *Enuma Eliš*) we read of TIAMAT:—

"She spawned monster-serpents,
Sharp of tooth and merciless of fang;
With poison instead of blood, she filled their bodies.
Fierce monster-vipers she clothed with terror.
Whoever beheld them, terror overcame them."

Returning to Lovecraft (Hay, *Necronomicon*):—

"Loathsome Cthulhu rose up from the Depths
and raged with exceeding great fury
against the Earth's Guardians: The Elder Gods."

And from the *Enuma Eliš*:—

"She acted possessed and lost her sense of reason..."

After the battle (*Necronomicon of H.P. Lovecraft*):—

"Beyond the Gate [to the Outside] dwell now the Old Ones;
not in the spaces known to men,
but in the angles between them..."

Hints of such "space between spaces" can also be found in the
Enuma Eliš:—

"Go and cut off the life of TIAMAT,
Let the wind carry her blood into *secret spaces.*"

Following this mythology, we can see why Simon chose the
"*Necronomicon*" as the form to present his "recension" of a Mar-
dukite-Babylonian grimoire. It was not a book of evil, but a book
of false perceptions concerning the Sumerian Anunnaki "*gods*"—
a picture painted by the priests dedicated to the "younger pantheon" of Mesopotamia, especially those emphasizing the
national god of Babylon: MARDUK. The attitude from Lovecraft
toward the book reveal it as dark and perverse; not meant for
the "realm of light" or "world of men," and instead to ever remain in the private collections of "select" men—who dared
never speak of it. Of course, Lovecraft's personal *Necronomicon*
was a work of pure fantasy, *but* cuneiform tablets composing the
oldest writings on the planet...*are not.* That such ancient Mesopotamian collections of these tablets now share a cover-name
with Lovecraft's creation is about the only debatable issue for
scholars and mystics alike, and one based purely on semantics of
a "title"—none of which actually changes the message. Peter
Levenda (allegedly "Simon") explains in a 2007 interview with
Tracy Twyman:—

"On another level: the *Necronomicon*—the publication of a
book called the *Necronomicon*—no matter what *Necronomicon* [version] it is; I think raises a lot of questions that have
become very controversial and that is: what is a true
'book'? Or, questions concerning the value of psuedoepi-
grapha; for instance, the *Key of Solomon* was not written by
'Solomon.' There's false attributions to it. The Gardnerian

Book of Shadows was written by Gerald Gardner. It wasn't written by some ancient pagan witches a thousand or even hundreds of years ago. So, we have to ask ourselves: where is the true value? The *Necronomicon* itself forces people to question: what do we really value? Do we value an ancient text because it's ancient? Or, do we value it because it has something else to offer us? Is a new text with an ancient patina just as valuable as a new text or a genuine ancient text? ...It asks a lot of questions."

The very application of "magic" to the system is a clue to savvy occult interpreters, since this magic of *sigil-forms, names* and *numbers* of Anunnaki *"gods,"* was "Mardukite-Hermetic"—specifically Babylonian and Chaldean—as passed down from *Enki.* The entire idea of "personal magic" is absent from the original pre-Babylonian religious system of Sumer. The most ancient Magicians, Priests, Priestesses and Kings, all maintained a direct relationship with the gods. Then later, after the gods "left earth," traditions of prayer and supplication became more prominent—the people sought to invoke the power of the (now) distant "gods" back into the material world. But nowhere in ancient Mesopotamian mysticism is there evidence for practices to "exorcise" power of the gods by *force*—making demands of the "divine" simply because some magicians is privy to a special name, signature or numeric formula. This "bolder" form of practice came about later during the neo-Babylonian and rise of Semitic cultures—it became popular in the Mediterranean as *"Hermetics"* and eventually came to dominate esoteric philosophies of Egypt and Greece. Francois Lenormant describes the origins and development of these beliefs:—

"The mystic name [*sign, seal, &tc.*] exercised a power upon the god himself to whom it belonged, and that when called by this name he was obliged to obey the incantation. The virtue of the formulae lay not in an invocation of the divine power, but in the fact of a man proclaiming himself such or such a God, and when he, in pronouncing the incantation, called to his aid any one of the various members of the pantheon, it was as one of themselves that he had a right to the assistance of his companions."

Marduk (and *Nabu*) taught this evolving methodology to magicians of his Hermetic magic (most likely against the wishes of his superiors)—the ability of assuming a "god-form" to compel the universe by magic, and to use incantations in his name, as found with a frequently used passage from the *Incantation of Eridu:*—

"*It is not I, but Marduk, who speaks the incantation.*"

Thus, magicians of the later systems spent more time divining secret names and formulas than establishing their own relationship with the powers they sought. Mystics of more antiquated traditions relied on "*true knowledge*" of the "*gods*" themselves—those possessing the very "names" and "numbers" of the cosmos. By petitioning the deity in self-honesty to act on their behalf, the Mesopotamian priest or priestess was able to perform works of utilitarian "magic" Positive "civic magic" aided development and maintenance of the land—the "*Realm*"—that lived and thrived under the patronage of a particular local Anunnaki deity). The original pursuit for power, by "magic," or favor of the gods, remains here, embedded within the ancient systems. Against popular belief, driven by fear and naivete, the ascent up the "Ladder of Lights" toward "god-hood" is no "Pandora's Box" waiting to harm the practitioner—the devouring will be only of one's impurity—for only the *Self-Honest* armed with *Absolute Truth* are allowed to pass, as Lenormant warns:—

"The power of magical incantation to compel obedience from the gods themselves became, however, formidable, even to him who exercised it, if he did not show himself worthy to possess it by moral purity and a knowledge of divine things."

"NOVEM PORTIS"
-or- THE NINE GATES OF THE KINGDOM OF SHADOWS

The path of the *Ancient Mystery Tradition* has, up until now, led the Seeker along a vast array of "colors" and "images"—up rungs of a *"Ladder of Lights"* as it were—tracing phantasmal images of the material world back to their Source. But, it is not glamorous procurement of further persona and personality upgrades that Seekers are after—rather, it is the absolution or dissolution of the same; transforming programming you have already acquired and become weights keeping you bound by distractions of—and energetic slavery to—the material very world; a Realm of *light* and *forms*.

So, a Seeker passes through *"Seven Gates of Life,"* questing for completion—to bring parts of the whole together—if they be so lucky. More often though, it is the case that initiates separate the *"whole"* into additional esoteric *"parts"* that merely ends with a life further separated—a spiral journey of vocabularies and paradigms, but no closer to the Source. Therefore, our emphasis should not be on the bedazzlement projected in front of our psyche for this world. An addiction quickly forms toward "intellectual delights—making some obscure *numerological* or *symbolic* links between a myriad of forms. But, the ALL is actually connected to *All* in systematic equality and oneness—not just to be found in a few sacred "correspondences"—these semantic relationships between observable attributes and invisible forces.

Wholeness. This is never fully realized in the World of Light that we are accustomed to. This world exists because of a state of perceived separation from the World of Darkness. Polarity. As a semantic solution, our purpose is not necessarily to glorify

Darkness, either. There are many people that succumb to trappings of Darkness, just as some do in the Light. Such only happens when the misinformed initiate is instructed to experience the ALL as "parts" *in exclusion* to other "parts." This occurs in many traditions emphasizing duality contrary to the Oneness that is the Source. Duality is not Oneness—and no system observing such can ever offer complete unification of cosmic knowledge.

So, what does one do? We first climb up the *"Ladder of Lights"*— on the *"Tree of Life"* we have fallen from—and thereby unify the manifold natures of existences found in the Light—but is this the end? While working back up the *"Tree of Life,"* the Seeker uncovers a very dangerous glitch in the system—that this is not all there is. But where is it? And how do we experience the hidden aspects of the cosmos for wholeness.

How do we get to the other side..?

The *"Master Astronomer Standing at the Gates of the Gods"* moves forth—traversing the Gates of this Universe. The Seeker inevitably moves passed the final doorway—the *"Seventh Gate"*— and is able to glean a look behind the curtain... And there is nothing more horrifying than what one will find. For indeed, all we have done and worked towards, all we have quested for in our endeavors through the Light and the material System, and when the curtain is peeled back it is only to reveal— Nothingness... *The Primordial Abyss.*

All of the systems in the mind—all that have gives form its meaning—has been washed away and the realization of the illusion is paralyzing. For when we had our *"Wizard of Oz"* to toy with in our minds, we could at the very least laugh in our own folly at being fooled into playing a game of some supernatural crazed madman behind the curtains. At the very least things could be made to make some sense—*systematically*—as a reflection of what we believe about the material world. But, now at the cusp of reality and sanity, we know better. Before you is the Other Side of the Tree... Crossing the Abyss... Into the Beyond... You have reached the edge...

You are have reached – *the Shadows...*

◊ ◊ ◊   ◊ ◊ ◊   ◊ ◊ ◊

After the rise of the *"Hermetic Order of the Golden Dawn"* and the "magical revival" in the late 1800', the spiritual and metaphysical world of the mystics—once hidden away, restricted to dank fens of society—began to appear in the public spotlight, or at least carry an *illusion* of being maintained in public view. With this followed the widespread revival and use of medieval grimoires—many of them translated or introduced by like *MacGregor Mathers* and Aleister Crowley. Magical organizations relating to these individuals—such as the GD (*Golden Dawn*), OTO (*Ordo Templi Orientis*) and Crowley's own AA (*Argentium Astrum*)—all begin to influence mystical practices and underground traditions, directly affecting the multitudes on the surface world.

Naturally, we are most concerned foremost with content from the Babylonian derived text—"*Necronomicon: The Anunnaki Bible*"—research and developed by the Mardukite Chamberlains in 2009—and its interconnected relationship to the Great Mysteries. However, the association of modern pseudoepigrapha in this regard is not limited simply to a book called the "*Necronomicon*"—for such is just a *name*, as is "*Al Azif,*" or anything else we want "*defined*" so as to give anything its definitive form. We often attempt to solidify that which cannot be solidified—that which is not meant to be solidified.

◊ ◊ ◊   ◊ ◊ ◊   ◊ ◊ ◊

The novel "*El Club Dumas*" released in Spain in 1993. American English-speaking audiences would have to wait three years to find "*The Club Dumas*" on their shelves. This literary treatment by *Arturo Perez-Reverte* was lost amidst a mystery genre ruled by more popular contemporaries like Agatha Christie and Sue Grafton. It did not receive considerable pop-culture attention until its motion picture realization under a different title.

In *Reverte*'s novel, the main character—*Corso*—set in a dusty environment of Antiquarian book-selling, is on a quest to uncover the truth of a lost fragment-chapter of the famous serial by Alexander Dumas—"*The Three Musketeers.*" In the course of events, Corso is culled into a different kind of quest... and more people have been exposed to the influence of this modern tale then you might originally suspect, for the cycle is known by another more popular title:

"*Nine Gates of the Kingdom of Shadows.*"

Although now popular in NexGen occultism, prior to the 2009 Mardukite "*Liber 9*" release (as "*Nine Gates of the Kingdom of Shadows*"), the work had previously escaped inevitable occult pseudoepigrapha! [Update: *Liber-9* materials are now incorporated into the Mardukite tablet catalog of "*Necronomicon: The Anunnaki Bible*" and are reprinted in this present anthology.]

From the Spanish edition we translate the title "*Nine Doors to the Kingdom of Darkness.*" We can appreciate the shift in American language—"*Gates*" become "portals," and "*Shadows*" changed to "*Darkness.*" These changes happen frequently with American cultural imports from other countries.

American audiences also seem more receptive to *video* media then books, as certainly motivated Roman Polanski to film "*The Ninth Gate,*" released in 1999, starring Johnny Depp. The wood-carved engravings that are so paramount to the film are taken directly from illustrations found in Reverte's novel.

It might surprise many occultists to note that the vein of pseudoepigrapha runs deep within the mystic stream— reaching down to all too familiar works, such as the "*Keys of Solomon*" or even the "*Book of Abramelin*"—genuine books with false assertions of authorship. It comes as no surprise that we see a rise of more legends of such "books within books"—"fantasies within fantasies"—as the existing human condition undoubtedly achieves its ends in the "*Realm of Light,*" when we must, by necessity of our survival, reach out to the *Shadows.*

Considering themes from the lore of *Nine Gates*, we are instructed that the work is based on yet another book—furthering our
psyche's journey an esoteric literary rabbit hole. The *"Delomelanicon"*—unarguably a new vision of the *Necronomicon* Cycle
—is a book reportedly written by the "Devil himself" as a guide
for "his followers." The work, said to have once been in the possession of King Solomon, reached the realm of Medieval Sorcery
in 1666 by *Aristide Torchia*, who published his version of this
"Devil's Notebook" as *"De Umbrarum Regni Novem Portis."*

Torchia and all but three copies of this work are burned by the
Church. The title—*"Delomelanicon"*—the current editor translates
as *"Book of Summoning the Darkness,"* (similar to the coveted, but
equally fantasy-based, witches' *Book of Shadows*). When first ana-
lyzed for *"Liber-9"* in 2009, some early Mardukite Chamberlains
preferred the translation *"Invocation of Darkness,"* as given in the
Soto translation of *"Club Dumas."*

If we lend a thought to this story for a moment, putting aside
trappings of semantics, vocabulary or verification of a medieval
sorcerer's grimoire—consider a book given to a class of followers from an entity contrary to the accepted "God On Duty"—
considered a *"devil"* to one side, and a *"savior"* to the other.

Immediately, we conjure to mind Anunnaki politics of ancient
Mesopotamia—beings like MARDUK and ENKI—or some other
specific "alien intelligence" with some motive for leading folks
back through the *Gates*. And if these beings are indeed hidden in
folds "between" the *"Realm of Light"*—the reality we see every-
day—then they would most certainly belong to the Shadows –
and the spaces between spaces.

The archetype conjured to mind by the *"Nine Gates"* is very similar to the *Necronomicon*. There is, at the very least, obvious
symbolic emphasis of "portals," "thresholds" and "gateways"—
such as is inseparably paramount to this lore. Following esoteric
and occult examples, the *"Gates"* are introduced to the Seeker
under the guise of "Darkness," because such was (and remains
to be) the perception of what is "forbidden" and "hidden" knowledge—at least from the perspective of the Realm of Light. For,

even as Peter Levenda concisely said of the Simon *Necronomicon*: "It is a book *about* Darkness." Levenda reiterates that it is not a book about "pacts with devils" or anything so trite, such as you might see with the *"Grand Grimoire"* (*"Red Dragon"*), &tc.—but more importantly it is an ancient, nearly prehistoric methodology for *understanding the Darkness*.

We can see by his choice of directing the *"Ninth Gate"* film, that Polanski is interested in the esoteric enigma of the *Necronomicon* —and what is interesting as a result: both Kenneth Grant and "Simon" have acknowledged *"The Ninth Gate"* in their works as nod in their direction. Without even knowing this, one can still easily compare the *"Ninth Gate"* movie to *"El Club Dumas"* and instantly recognize where the emphasis shift lies. Simon, in his book *"Dead Names"* explains that—

> "...anyone who met me in those days in the 1970's would recognize Johnny Depp's character: glasses, beard, black clothes, black raincoat, bag over one shoulder. The intrigue that follows some of the events in the real story [of the publication of the Simon *Necronomicon*] including the references to wealthy individuals who sought the power of the book for themselves."

Those already familiar with the *"other side"* of the Mystery Tradition have possibly run across the cryptic O.T.O. series of three trilogies produced by Kenneth Grant. The final volume of this sequence of literature—*"The Ninth Arch"*—released in 2002, three years after the *"Ninth Gate"* movie (and a decade after the release of *"El Club Dumas"*). The current editor's opinion is only that one title bore some resemblance of the other. In Grant's case, the designation of "Arch" carried dual meanings—both to an idea of "Gateways," but also semantic parallels (something Grant is obsessed with in his writings) between the words *"Arch"* and *"Arachnid"*—AR*a*CH*nid*.

So now, thanks to Kenneth Grant, we have the "Spider" to add to the equation—as he offers *"Ninth Arch"* as the *"Book of the Spider"* or *"Grimoire of the Spider."* The *"Grimoire of the Night"* and other obscure works by the author, focus on the "other side of the Tree"—once the initiate has first worked through the "*Grim-oire of the Light.*" [These Spider transmissions are designated in the O.T.O. as both "*Book 29*" and "OKBISh"—a name Grant claims is related to a Mesopotamian root for word "Spider."]

A lifetime can be spent chasing fragmented rays of light glimmering in various magical schools, but, all of this suggests that beneath the surface of the light, and in the "*betweens,*" there is as yet another part to the mystery for the Seeker—the "*Darkness*"—the "*Shadows.*" In most cases, the Seeker will just rush to throw light against the screen again, impressing familiar images from their own experiences in the Light—not allowing the self-honest experience of something "unknown" to unfold. We need not materialize demonic images or cast fears before us only to allow them to become manifest by our own will—as such is not the true nature of the Shadows. Such falseness has only been created within the fragmented and fractured minds of men who further the polar necessity for the Shadows as they cling to the Light.

For what greater horror could man behold in the Realm of Light, then to reach the unspeakable realization that is most capable of shattering their delicate human psyche (and perhaps the dissolution of the Ego)—that it is no demon or gruesome vision to behold—but the full experience that the material world is a mere veil to something else. It is not the ends in itself, only but a *means.*

But how can reality come apart at the seams? For, we are a nation of civilized and enlightened men, are we not? Surely even humans have come to take the gear-grinding world for granted and the systems and boundaries that keep things in "check" are also in fear of dissolution—including monetary and political—as even *George Hay* notes, in his Preface to the "*R'lyeh Text,*" concerning world changes taking place on the planet since the *Necronomicon* cycle and early "Mardukite" revival of the 1970's noting:—

   "... the dissolution of 'fixed' and 'given' groupings of Na-tion-States, and, far more important, of the belief systems that had until recently been holding them together."

Considering that the Lightworkers have further taken their fragmented human psyche and placed greater limits and sanctions of "good" and "evil" on all existence, the perpetuation of duality continues unresolved in the universe. With only casual interpretation of Mardukite *Necronomicon* lore—one might say that mankind was separated from the "Source," for an existence in a polarized world. But humans also further this separation from the Source over the course of their lives by lengthening the distance between perceived opposites instead of seeking harmony—*a return to the Source.* So long as the separation is maintained in the mind, manifestations of fear, jealousy, discord and the like will continue to be given existence in reality and confirmed by the psyche. While progression on the "spiral of evolution" is always forward and upward—the speed and rate of travel (or development of our spiritual evolution) is not guaranteed by any tradition not standing in *Self-Honesty.*

THE SIMON NECRONOMICON

The most widely distributed of all known versions of the *Necro-nomicon* is an edition released under editorship of simply the name "Simon." If you are currently reading this book, you are probably already familiar with the version of which I refer. Originally released in 1977 (then re-released in 2008) as a prestigious hardcover format, it is the mass-market paperback edition by Avon books (now HarperCollins) that received most of the attention by occultists and skeptics alike.

According to Simon, in *"Dead Names"*—his own account of the *"Dark History of the Necronomicon"*—the paperback edition, first released in 1980, has now sold nearly one-million copies (as of 2010), not including those innumerable versions recirculated by electronic and illegal means online and through unauthorized self-publishing. However, success of this printing history in the occult genre has only been rivaled by the work of *Anton LaVey*, also published by Avon Books—though it is important to note that LaVey's work started reaching mainstream markets in 1969, over a decade before the *Necronomicon* paperback.

Simon's *Necronomicon* might have made a sooner public appearance, but as the story goes, they had difficulties finding the right publisher for it in the mid-1970's. The "Cthulhu Mythos" drew a growing subculture of cult-fiction fans into the *Necronomicon* archetype (from writings of H.P. Lovecraft), but it seemed that no one really wanted to touch the project—either they weren't being taken seriously (or were afraid to), or it was just assumed that the project was doomed to fail.

As anyone who has professionally worked with anything related to publication of a *Necronomicon* might understand, the actual truth of the situation is somewhere in the middle.

Literary creators have two choices when confronted with development and production barriers—either abandon the notion altogether or do it yourself. Those of us who have felt strongly enough about our "place" in the mysteries—and who have not been "blessed" with soul-selling spiritual contracts to blatant commercial success, and are self-honestly determined enough to see the work through (in spite of personal discord and suffering that often results from "arts-in-commerce-driven-by-passion") —take it upon ourselves, in the Shadows of the mainstream, on our own tenacity, to do what we feel we must... *Against all odds.*

Sadly, it is only when manifested art and literary creations are brought out of the "shadows" that it becomes the subject of public scrutiny, in the public—in the Realm of Light—where occult work does not belong in the first place. This presents a serious "spiritual" or "mystical" dilemma, one confronted by nearly every "secret society" or "occult organization" that has been charged to hold any true aspect of the mysteries—how to deal with the publicly written word?

During the 1970's, bringing books to print of this caliber was a serious feat. It was a different age and time from what we have grown accustomed to today—and likewise, taken for granted. Things were done by mail and by phone—things took longer. We were not living in the current "print-on-demand" age where nearly any self-proclaimed "author" can now see their book "in print"—for a small price. Books were still being "typeset." Equipment and efforts were different and computers were not what they are today (or even always available to the average citizen). If you were not already a part of the "big publishing" industry, the labor, equipment and materials were not readily at your disposal or economical.

What is only loosely spoken of in pop-culture metaphysical literature and occult manuals is the "power" exercised simply in such mass amounts of energy moving—and when done intentionally, these efforts in themselves can render projects with "life," not even considering what occurs when it reaches the "reality" of someone beyond the originator(s).

Of all esoteric versions of "*Necronomicon*" found on the market today, the predecessor *is* the Simon work, not including the very loose and scattered references from Lovecraftian literature decades earlier. A lesser known version by George Hay appeared in the underground shortly thereafter. The two were completely unconnected—as the Seeker often finds when comparing the many available versions—other than use of a title and theme: "*Necronomicon.*"

When Simon's *Necronomicon* first debuted, very few people were privy to this specific "type" of esoteric understanding. It concerned a truly archetypal, pre-classical and pre-Christian methodology—a root system from which many other branches of the tree later formed, then perceived as separate—whether because of semantics or their cultural locale in time and geography. Even many supposed occultists and New Agers of the period had very little background in the real mythos being dealt with—which was not at all *Lovecraftian*, or even *Sumerian* as many others believe, but *Babylonian!*—the original ancient "Mardukite" paradigm.

The "Mardukite paradigm" is not paramount to any other popular editions of the "*Necronomicon*," including the Hay edition and also contributions of ritual magician, Donald Tyson —all of which are based purely on the vision and semantics of H.P. Lovecraft's "stories." It should be made clear that the "Mardukite Core" is not based on fundamentals or semantics present in the "Lovecraftian" paradigm; it is Mesopotamian—specifically, Babylonian.

With the arrival of Simon's *Necronomicon* and its relationship with the work of *H.P. Lovecraft* (based on the title alone), the two mythoi have been confused by neo-gothic punks and "emo"-musicians as being one and the same. And although there is no real correlation to the work of Anton LaVey (other than being simultaneously produced by the same publisher), based on its marketed image alone, the "Simon" book is just as often found in the hands of someone carrying Anton LaVey works on "Satanism"—and as such the *Simon* book received further dark shadowy undertones as a result.

Contents aside, it may be that the manifestation of a tangible book, wholly obscure for its time, with the title across the front —NECRONOMICON—is what really launched the success of the book. For many, the chances to own and possess a work of such epic proportions was a dream come true. But as with many dreams and wishes, the dreamer does not always know what is for their own higher good. The only thing sometimes more daunting than the *quest* itself—is when you actually *find* what you seek!

One is then left to wonder: if the title used to label the work has been fabricated and is, in itself, the product of a fictional work by the hands of *Lovecraft*, to what validity might there even be to the *Simon* work using the title? Such is really an ignorant question, for the true Seeker should not be so easily caught up in missing the forest for the trees. Again, the Truth Seeker is urged to disregard that *one* semantic for their pursuit into genuine Mesopotamian mysteries, in order to have a self-honest experience on the pathway—not one that is so easily tainted by arbitrary filters put in your way to cause a distraction from any true 'enlightenment'.

Due to the "left-handed magical" embrace of the *Cthulhu Mythos* drawn from writings of *H.P. Lovecraft*, the "*Simon Necronomicon*" is marketed (and often boasted by practitioners of "New Age" traditions) as a powerful book of "black magick," a "grimoire of evil sorcery" and the "most dangerous book" in existence!

No sooner had Simon's *Necronomicon* been celebrated for coming into being, it was just as quickly *denounced* for its existence—and not exclusively by the right-wing types that you would normally expect, mind you—but, by the very pulp-fiction fans who originally anticipated, then rejoiced in its arrival! Surely, this was *not* the "*Necronomicon*" originally referred to by Lovecraft!

... And thank the gods for that!

Experience is wholly subjective—a matter of perspective—and the written word is often communication of experience from a perspective by the author. This is actually how history is manipulated throughout the ages. True communication is dependent on its *receivers* and "instructors" of this history to have the ability to paint experiences of the "unknown past" without their own biases.

Subsequent generations carrying this communication have, in effect, shaped the way humans interact with their world—based on their "worldview." The *Necronomicon* is a paradigm or a "worldview," reflecting some of the oldest known beliefs and traditions on the planet—alluding to things that can very much *affect* the unprepared. That the uninitiated, who is already unstable, risks their own delicate psyche when "dabbling" in lore better left to others, is very much the case—but not necessarily any more the case with the *Necronomicon* then anything else. We all know these types. If they weren't able to attribute their "madness" to the *Necronomicon*, they would just as soon be fundamentalist victims of some other creed. The difference is, the *Necronomicon* gnosis represents the "truth behind the world" hidden in the shadows and darkness of man's common worldview today—it becomes an easy target for attack. Because of its tangible absence, but century of allusions, its reputation preceded it—*heavily*.

When experienced from the dualistic perspective common to con-temporary reality, the *Necronomicon* does seem to represent a "dark element" in the spectrum. Part of this relates simply to the title and gothic overtones related to "death." Another part is the actually methodology involved. It represents aspects of our history that have been hidden from us, misrepresented, and— once we find out the truth behind even the system it is based in —shrouded in deception. It alludes even further to an understanding of existence that requires no degrees, titles or magick words and is instead dependent on true and faithful individualized experience of the "*Abyss*," a Void-of-Naught—the Infinity of Nothingness—which just so happens to be the true background existence to material reality—everywhere and nowhere at once.

Based on modern "Mardukite" Babylonian research, the *Necronomicon* paradigm becomes a very serious subject—well beyond

Lovecraftian fantasies—that many "blessed" with involvement in this necessary paradigm-shift for our times, take very seriously. Unlike many *Necronomicon* critics out there who simply scream "hoax" to anything that bares the title, the modern "Mardukite" institution is more sympathetic toward early changes in consciousness provided by Simon's contribution—even if incomplete when compared to the greater encompassing "Mardukite" tradition.

Skeptical critics are used to throwing out the baby with the bath-water, without giving things a second thought. For them, the content of the Simon's *Necronomicon* itself—or even "*Necronomicon: The Anunnaki Bible*" for that matter—is irrelevant, given that the *title* of the work may be derived from a fictional source. Even though the interior corpus of the text has no real relationship with "*Lovecraftian*" fiction, it is easier for them to disregard the whole thing altogether, over a title. And these are the same "high minds" that would in another breath urge you "not to judge a book by its cover" (and so on) and yes, the same minds that so many other naïve initiates turn to for their *answers*.

◊ ◊ ◊   ◊ ◊ ◊   ◊ ◊ ◊

Most work on the "Simon" grimoire seems to have been handled by a man named *Peter Levenda*, who has actually remained the primary public face for any "Simon" work—regardless of who "Simon" may actually be. It is interesting to note that combined, the name Simon-Peter is actually significant—in biblical context, where Simon becomes "Saint Peter," as the "Rock of the Church." Since mutual acquaintanceship connects the modern *Mardukite Research Organization* with the original *Simon* circle, protection of individual identities and associations is essential—not only when dealing with Mystery Traditions (as has always been the case), but especially when dealing with the *Necronomicon*. In short—*a lot* of underground politics is involved.

There are many issues with presenting Simon's *Necronomicon* as a historical book in itself. Firstly, the original manuscript it is supposed to be based on was stolen not long after copies were made for translation. And even these copies seem to be unavailable to anyone now. More important for our purposes than dating any actual manuscript, is dating the tradition which alluded to. Materials from Simon's *Necronomicon* bare striking resemblance to information derived from other available books of esoteric archeology, including—*"Semitic Magic," "Chaldean Magic"* and *"Babylonian Magic."*

The one thing it is not—it is *not* Sumerian in origin, as many thought and as its own editors profess. While it is true that Sumerians occupied the same space geographically linked to its birth-place—and they observed the same basic "Anunnaki" pantheon—their tradition is not actually evident in the work other than what was culturally absorbed into later traditions Simon's work is actually based—*Babylon.* Any idea that this tradition is "nondenominational" is also false. It is clearly laced with the "Mardukite-specific" spiritual politics found strongest in Babylonian traditions and literature—and often mirrored in Egypt. Among these themes, of course—a centralized veneration of MARDUK-RA as the "Lord of the Gods," something entirely absent in the previous (original) *Sumerian Tradition.*

According to the story provided in *"Dead Names,"* the manuscript that served as a basis for Simon's *Necronomicon* was allegedly recovered from a stolen rare-book collection in 1972. Those later involved with translation and presentation of the salvaged tome were none other than aforementioned Peter Levenda, and also *Herman Slater,* the owner of Magickal Childe bookstore in Manhattan, originally known as the Warlock Shop.

Completed and dedicated on October 12, 1975 (the hundredth anniversary of *Aleister Crowley*'s birth), the book required another two years of work before the team successfully brought it to the public. One common misconception is that *Magickal Childe* published Simon's *Necronomicon* in hardcover, when its production was actually managed as a somewhat private venture under the umbrella name: *Schlangekraft, Inc.* Later, however, *Magickal Childe* is credited with release of the first edition of a slim sequel volume, originally called the *Necronomicon Report,* then republished more widely as Simon's *"Necronomicon Spellbook,"* first appearing in the underground in 1981, then later reprinted by Avon (now HarperCollins).

As mentioned, self-publishing books during the mid-1970's required some serious skill and experienced people—and *money!* In walks *Larry Barnes* to the *Magickal Childe* bookstore—a man with a lifelong obsession with all things Lovecraft and an undying desire to publish and promote a *"Necronomicon."* Some other caretakers of the original manuscript or those involved with the project—declining acknowledgment for this current Mardukite volume—claimed to care little (or know nothing about) H. P. Lovecraft, although most swear that the title did actually grace the manuscript cover—but *not* the familiar sigil, which was apparently created later, as with the remaining art for the book, including the interior "sigils." The title remains the main questionable aspect related to the presentation of the book in public. Other than the "energy" that the name caries, the title alone really says nothing definitive toward the validity of its contents.

That it was a stolen manuscript seems plausible. That it does, in fact, bare renderings of the little-known (at the time) tablet invocations and epics from Mesopotamia—we have already established in our Mardukite *Necronomicon* cycle. That a practical "Sumerian Tradition" revival was of supreme interest, but previously inaccessible, to Aleister Crowley and the O.T.O. "magical organization" is also on record. The idea that the *title* may have been adopted later by request, or to offer the work substance—a canvas to be set against—may have actually been the only real fabrication. The title alone is all that Larry Barnes cared about when he wanted to make a "real" bound-book version of the *"Necronomicon"*—if the content seemed historically valid, then even better.

Book design was left to *James ("Jim") Wasserman*, who had previously worked for a prestigious occult bookseller—*Samuel Weiser*. Jim was in charge of seeing the actual design and construction of the book through. These same public entities connected to Simon's *Necronomicon* have—over three decades later—re-released the hardcover in late 2008, for its *31st Anniversary*—the same year that we officially founded the modern "Mardukite" movement. Wasserman returned to present a leather-bound edition exclusively from Studio 31, limited to 220 copies. The standard cloth-bound unlimited edition remains available as distributed by Ibis—the more recently established Samuel Weiser publishing imprint dedicated to hardcover editions. In 1977, the original leather-bound editions (numbered of 666) sold for $50 each. Today, these limited editions can fetch several hundred dollars up to a thousand. Comparatively, the newer 2008 cloth-bound hardcover edition retailed for $125—with Studio 31 offering its limited leather editions for $295. They have become as collectible to some now as they are sacred to others.

"Cthonic" presentation of the book and the dark gloom tied to the project did little to divert the "dread" and "horror" already attached to the title. Ornate cover design on the original hardcover met the preference of Larry Barnes, seeking again to define that *grimoire* from Lovecraft's visions. "Simon" writes in *Dead Names* that he would have preferred simpler cover—something they certainly achieved with the more frugal 2008 edition. The developers followed ideas put forth in Lovecraft's work more than they emphasized the specific content drawn from Mesopotamia. Simon's *Necronomicon* was presented as an archetypal long-lost sorcerer's "black book," the "most dangerous and powerful" on the planet—at least for its time. In some ways, the hype was justified. Certainly monumental for its time, the work remains a cornerstone for many today—although its efforts have since been surpassed by the work of the *Mardukite Research Organization*—specifically *"Necronomicon: The Anunnaki Bible"* and its supporting materials.

Very few—even those who had studied cultural folk mythologies and other pagan pantheons revived by "mystical movements" of the last century—had gained any access to (or understanding of) the ancient Mesopotamian methodologies predating all the rest. This change in human consciousness was not only monumental, but intentional—an integral part of a larger picture where obscure spiritual forces and secret councils have indeed been directing the course of many events in recent history. These include some many profound ventures from the 1970's, bridging the 60's to the 80's via visions and manifestations that many might have never conceived of before. The music changed. The media changed. The very colors being perceived in the world changed – more real, surreal and yet wholly artificial. Ground work began in human consciousness. A new *Babylon*—a new *Mardukite* age—was *rising*.

The technological age was counter-balanced with an extreme sense of "fantasy" and "spiritual occultism," such as had not been present in human civilization for a very long time. It was a necessary program, followed to temper the rise of the "electronic gods"—those that are still being raised to supremacy by their human creators. Thinking that the "*Old Gods*" have left them, humans have felt an overwhelming need to raise another in its place—this time, by their own creation—or so they think. It was not until fantasy enthusiasts and Lovecraftian *Necronomicon* readers started getting together with the science-fiction and Sitchin-eqsue circles in the late 1970's that the "mainstream population" (outside of orders like the *Golden Dawn* or *O.T.O.*) were given a chance to understand what was already known in the remote underground for thousands of years—knowledge concerning the existence and nature of the *Anunnaki!*

Most controversy surrounding Simon's *Necronomicon* concerned its presentation as H.P. Lovecraft's *Necronomicon*, and further as a "dreaded tome" that held power from the start, based on some of the more "supernatural" claims dealing with its production. Among these—that the typesetters were plagued by a swarm of rats during their work—an aspect that seems to bother a lot of critics. Things of this nature do little to affect the actual content, but the idea being brought forth, again, was—"this book is *dangerous!*" The debate about rats in factories seems so trite compared to the bigger picture and is it really that bizarre at any rate—we are talking about Manhattan, right? That the book might "expose you to psychological forces with which you cannot cope" is also not an empty boast. If you are not ready to face the reality that everything you think you know about your world is a sham—a clever deception by alien forces—then certainly, steer clear of the *Necronomicon* in all of its forms.

THE SCHLANGEKRAFT
RECENSION

Modern revival of ancient ideologies—known as the *"New Age Movement"*—has successfully brought new public awareness to many ancient mythoi. Consider: folk traditions of Europeans in the guise of neodruidism or Celtic witchcraft; resurgence in use of Norse runes and divination systems of Romany gypsies; "singing bowls" from Buddhist monks and Tibetan shamanism; a cornucopia of Asian *feng shui* devices—all these things litter aisles of nearly every "metaphysical" outlet. Furthermore, there is no shortage of statuary and holy regalia that can be purchased to grace devotional altar spaces of contemporary ceremonialists.

Preceding all of this—distant remains of the most ancient energetic currents of the cosmos. These were later interpreted somewhat differently by varying regional cultures throughout time—cultures that are relatively more recent and thus seem more accessible for modern revival. Absent among these many avenues—a means where the Seeker is offered their best assistance in returning to the Source—to long-lost forgotten tablets of Mesopotamia. These ancient cuneiform tablets are only recently being shaken free enough of the sands they were lost to, for them to finally be seen self-honestly again from out of the underground... Even if only glimmers and glimpses can be caught from early efforts in the 1970's.

Peter Levenda connects origins of Simon's *Necronomicon* to a little known *Slavonic Orthodox Church*. After discovering many covert political atrocities to the *Church's* involvement, *Levenda* says he defected from this mode of life, seeking to separate himself from its corruption. But, he was present long enough to see other established sects and churches rise and intertwine with their own brand, contributing higher legitimacy to otherwise shady and "unsavory" characters.

Two shady individuals notorious for rare-book theft—whose identities are never actually revealed—allegedly came in contact with *Levenda* and the *Church* at one juncture. These men made their living by going into libraries, universities and other private collections and literally stealing books. Some books had maps and diagrams that could be spliced and sold separately for even higher returns then what the entire work might be worth in tact. Sometimes methods were even employed to "raising seals," hiding ownership by libraries, &tc., and rebinding and re-pairing old books, when necessary, for resale. A significant collection of occult materials made its way into possession of founding members of the *Slavonic Orthodox Church*, which *Peter Levenda* became privy to while working and visiting with col-leagues. From this collection came forth the famous Simon's *Necronomicon*.

Simon's *Necronomicon* was quickly absorbed into "counter-cul-ture" and mistaken as some kind of devil-worshiping companion to LaVey's Satanism; which is just as often misunderstood, but beyond the scope of our current subject. The Simon work has never been readily accepted into the—now mainstream—"New Age." It is less frequently integrated into modern magical traditions of "legitimate" practicing *Wiccans* and *Druids*, and more often found among teenagers and young adults with no occult background—not to mention those up-and-coming in the "*Matrix*-generation." These "NexGens" are fully aware of the concept that they are living in some *Tron*-like computer game reality. NexGens know it is not only possible—now they can show you just how it is done and how we might make it work for us—burrowing the rabbit-hole ever deeper—fragmenting the path back to the Source.

By fragmenting the puzzle into more pieces, the chase to put the picture back together becomes longer, more challenging—and to the psyche that is driven by stimulus—more intriguing. With more pieces to the puzzle there are more ways in which parts *might* be "fit together" and "connected" to give that psyche its much needed fix of "eureka" (yet another glamour). Keep in mind that the size, nature and picture for the puzzle (the "big picture") remain fixed—only the number of pieces and level of difficulty are changed.

But, the occult is what it is for a reason. It holds just as many glamours and illusions as the *"Realm of Light"* people are more comfortably familiar with. The true secrets of the "occult lodge" protect themselves, even when out in the open—and publishing words does not guarantee esoteric understanding. It is far easier to hide something in front of someone and keep them going on the notion that what they seek requires additional seeking— more levels and layers of understanding. This is essentially what has become an "enlightenment deception" on the surface world, or what many philosophers might simply call *"false knowledge."*

The *Necronomicon*—both in archetype and form—represent a way out of *this* trapping. ...But! Without guidance (such as expressed in more recent Mardukite efforts—including *"Necronomicon: The Anunnaki Bible"* and the current Mardukite *"Gates of the Necronomicon"* cycle of material)—the Seeker is inevitably just going to fall into trappings of a different system, and this time possibly not make it *out*. Why? Because it was designed to be that way. Those who have worked through the "initiatory program" of the *"Gates"* from the Simon version will many times over tell themselves they have been "successful," even though they still are experiencing it from a "first degree" realization. Then there are those who have stumbled into the niche of the system, and arrived in the *Abyss*. This is rare—and still only a fraction of what the whole system represents – a mere *shadow*.

◊ ◊ ◊   ◊ ◊ ◊   ◊ ◊ ◊

One modern occultist bridging the gap between Aleister Crowley's era and the modern one—*Kenneth Grant*. Some of Grant's earlier works could only allude to possible connections between Crowley's "magick" and specifically Lovecraftian interpretations of "*Necronomicon.*" In recent installments of Grant's "Typhonian O.T.O." materials, he begins citing from what he calls the "*Schlangekraft recension*"—otherwise known as Simon's *Necronomicon*.

Of Kenneth Grant's many cryptic tomes composing the "Typhonian Tradition" of *Ordo Templi Orientis*, the one titled "*Outer Gateways*," briefly describes communications made by ceremonial magicians of magical lodges with the "*Old Ones*" or "*Deep Ones*"—demonstrating that he evidently took this subject seriously. Kenneth Grant essentially inherited the O.T.O. organization and cult-following of Aleister Crowley. Therefore, we can be certain that the *Schlangekraft recension* was far from the only means—or even remotely close to their original experiments—of making contact with "alien intelligences." But Grant acknowledged—no doubt made successful use of—and celebrated the work as a very real "*Portal to the Abyss*." The book represented an element—Mesopotamia—that earlier magicians weren't accessing directly with any of their systems, as Peter Levenda expresses in an interview:—

> "Where the New Age is concerned, a lot of the occultism is 'Judeo-Christian'—the *Keys of Solomon*, for example; the *Secret Books of Moses*, and all of that stuff. It was all based on a *Jewish* and *Christian* concept. With the coming of the New Age you did have a rise in neopaganism, but there was not a system of 'ceremonial magick' for a neopagan mentality; it [ceremonial magick] was, again, based on *Jewish* and *Christian* concepts, which were themselves borrowed from pagan origins, but the pagan origins were gone for the most part. In a sense the *Simon Necronomicon* filled a need for people with a true neo-pagan interest to become involved with the *higher magics*."

Rather than a "Cthulhu mythos" drawn from semantics used by H. P. Lovecraft to describe his dreams and visions, the *Schlangekraft recension* offered a preliminary means for someone with no background in Mesopotamian cultures or ancient cuneiform tablets to quickly immerse themselves—thereby unlocking a personal subconscious "portal" to the "*Other*." The work is by no means complete and certainly not wholly accurate, but that is not to say it has not served its purpose in the greater scheme —in the system—just as the contributions of others, intricately interwoven, have as well. Kenneth Grant notes in "*Outside the Circles of Time*" that:—

"Certain fugitive elements appear occasionally in the works of poets, painters, mystics and occultists which may be regarded as genuine magical manifestations in that they demonstrate the power and ability of the artist to evoke elements of an extra-dimensional and alien universe that may be captured only by the most sensitive and delicately adjusted antennae of human consciousness..."

That Simon's *Necronomicon* is not representative of Sumerian *paradigms* is already apparent and will continue to be demonstrated as such here. The type of dualism suggested—the supremacy of MARDUK—are all very clear indicators of Chaldeo-Babylonian "Mardukite" elements not found in early Sumer.

The Simon book *is not* a proper "priest's guide" for even following the traditions and paradigm of Mardukite Babylon—as such, the Mardukite work (and what is presented within this anthology) was developed. Instead, Simon's book is presented as a bastardized magician's "grimoire," primarily describing ritual-styled sorcery more common to "Hermetic magic," but not the religious or ceremonial "priestly" methods that we should expect to be present. The manner in which forces are dealt with indicates a perspective of someone slightly "outside" the original Mardukite system—someone who is not personally in a position to relay it fully, for they have not been fully initiated to it themselves.

References in Simon's book to "*Enki, Our Father*" is another key Mardukite Babylonian sign-post. A purely Sumerian tradition would have heralded divine attributes primarily to *Enlil,* and then perhaps also to his heir-son *Ninurta.* Instead, it is Babylonian in origin, deferring all esoteric powers of "earthly magic" and "world order" specifically to *Enki,* and his own heir-son *Marduk*—the patron *Anunnaki* deity of Babylon. In both the modern Mardukite "*Necronomicon: The Anunnaki Bible*" and Simon's *Necronomicon,* "ANU" remains a distant figure and *Enlil* is only mentioned occasionally—in regard to the "Supernal Trinity." The ancient Mardukite Babylonians assigned all worldly "Enlil-ship" or "God-ship" to *Marduk*—and "*on earth as it is in heaven.*"

Before any planetary "*Gates*" are introduced in the *Schlangekraft Recension*, the introductory "Testimony of the Mad Arab" describes an unnumbered "*Gate of Death*" called GANZIR. Lore of this Gate exists from cuneiform tablet epics describing crossings specifically to the "Underworld," but it is not necessarily the "*Gate to the Outside*" or to the "*Abyss*" that is alluded to elsewhere —it is not the "Gate-to-End-All-Gates." It is not part of the "*Ladder of Lights*" because it is not a part of the visible "*Realm of Light*" and it is not "realized" in the seven-fold "stargate-system" of Mardukite Babylon for this reason—nor is the "*Earth Gate*" or the "*Supernal Trinity*" stations—all of which were combined to form later "kabbalistic" representations of this system.

The more familiar sevenfold web-matrix represents the "seven rays" (or "seven pillars") used specifically to seal systems of the physical, material, manifest and visible world. The "*Gate of Ganzir*" does not lead "out of the system," but rather it links to the *Underverse* domain of *Ereshkigal* and *Nergal*—a dimly lit part of the same system, but the "*Other Side*" of the Tree of Life. Rather than a vast palette of colors for material manifestation, the *Underworld* is fashioned by an "absence" of these colors—a pale reflection in *shadows*—but it is not the "No-Being-Void-Nothingness" found in the *Abyss*. It is said: Death is merely a threshold state—a crossing—but you are still not there! Why, then, is such lore even alluded to in the texts if it is not being directly utilized in the gate-system? Answer:—To fully enlighten the initiate (Seeker) to the magnitude of what they are dealing with: that the *Anunnaki* forces hold the keys to both life and death—because both are still a part of dualistic existence—fractal entities —fragmented from the whole into individualized existence.

Ceremonialists raised in elitist traditions are eventually aware of the short circuit that is embedded in their own highly elevated systems—spread out through countless tomes and journals of spiritual theories and mystic entanglement. Having chanted all the combinations of syllables and added all the *gematric* numbers, they are left back alone in their lavishly decorated circles successful in only conjuring a protection against true enlightenment and their own fears. This is probably what intrigued Kenneth Grant the most about the *Schlangekraft recension*, for its esoteric emphasis was not on the Realm of Light, but the "Realm of Death," naturally overshadowing the work from the start— beginning with the very title: *Necronomicon*.

A long-standing history of "death-cult" themes connected to the *Necronomicon*-archetype spark reservations for many folk— preventing new insights—again, mainly due to the title. The same facets that blindly attracted over a million people to its pages are what keeps countless times that many away. They are unaware of what the "Mesopotamian" work really entails—the contents and deeper gnosis of ancient mysteries that it actually can provide. For that matter, many who own or come across the book are intrigued, even inspired by its existence, but are afraid to read it themselves, following a stereotyped "urban-legend" begun by H. P. Lovecraft, that the mere reading can cause madness. All the better. Such minds really should not delve into the occult anyways, as there is not enough holy water and blessed salt in existence to keep their fears from eventually manifesting—creating more problems for the rest of us.

As we might expect, Kenneth Grant's O.T.O. approach is meta-physical rather than literal, recognizing "death" as a transitional "crossing." In fact, he semantically correlates "death" with *"Daath,"* the hidden *"sephiroth"* ["sphere," "sta-tion" or "gate"] in the later Semitic Kabbalah, derived from the same Babylonian gate-system as the *Necronomicon*. The Kabbalah depicts "Daath" as an "eleventh" factor in an otherwise tenfold system, barely visible from *this side* of the "Tree of Life" and somehow bridging the world of "form" to a realm of "not"—a Gateway to Voidness. It is not "voidness" in itself, but an embed-ded loophole in the system dividing the height or summit of the lower material (physical) existence from the foundation or depths of the higher Supernal (spiritual) existence. Understand that all existence [AN.KI] is, of course, a singular reality, it has merely been fixed with curtains and doors, veils and gates, by which it might be more easily contained...

and it works pretty well.

TOWARDS A BABYLONIAN NECRONOMICON

Everyone coming in contact with the "Necronomicon paradigm" has come and gone preaching their own personal truths about it. For many, it is a fictitious manifestation that could not ever be real. Others see it as part of the "*Akashic Libraries*," an account that is locked away in the astral, just waiting for some person to unlock the mysteries.

There are some who find the appeal to fantasy and horror, but they do not believe themselves or anyone else capable of discerning the truth or exercising real power. Too often it is the highly inquisitive analytic human minds that breathe life into spiritual-semantic stumbling blocks. But—as reality is a matter of perspective, each "viewpoint" is only correct from a certain "point of view." Consider this as we move through this lesson.

Firstly, modern "grimoires" directly influenced by H. P. Lovecraft (*Hay & Tyson*) can hardly be considered "genuine" articles of ancient literature and mysticism in themselves—and so we will not spend much space and time here to analyze them. Most Lovecraftian-inspired creations (*Hay/Turner & Tyson*) are usually designed by not only enthusiastic fans of Lovecraft, but also experienced "ceremonial magicians," who already carry an understanding of "grimoire-magic" operations. Therefore, they have a good chance of creating a workable system of magic that will yield positive results for others—as much as any other. *If you build it, they will come.*

It is not difficult for experienced practitioners to construct their own workable systems—especially those spending many years immersed in correspondence tables and comparative charts of elemental and planetary forces.

All these system require is a "theme" or "pantheon"—some structure to base the "vibrations" and "rays" against. If a suitable one is not found, or able to be conjured from readily available cultural research, the next option is to just *make one up*. As Timothy Leary suggested—*"start your own religion"*—and in the case of Lovecraft's fanatics, *they did just that*. In essence the forces are already in place namelessly operating by the same Cosmic Laws—they await only to be named and known by a subjective individuated psyche. Hence for Lovecraftians: the *Cthulhu Mythos!*

While the "Simon group" worked to "translate" (or "develop") the *Schlangekraft recension* in New York, another *Necronomicon*—also an independent "first" of its kind—was simultaneously being edited and designed on the other side of the Atlantic Ocean, in England. As much as Simon's work brought the legendary archetype to life as an influence for the rising *"Mardukite Age"* and specifically dedicated to the *Anunnaki* energy-currents of *Marduk*, the U.K. team (*George Hay, Robert Turner* and *Colin Wilson*) were far more interested in allegorical power embedded in Lovecraft's own archetypal *egregores*—specifically the *"Cthulhu Mythos"* in exclusion to all else.

Where once we had no *Necronomicons*, by the end of the 1970's the world now had three—including an *H. R. Giger* art book.

George Hay's *"Necronomicon: Book of Dead Names"* appeared in 1978. The work did not initially see much attention beyond underground circulation—as is common of these types of releases at their inception—but it did provoke a more serious occult revival interest toward Lovecraftian-specific semantics. The book was only distributed in the United States after being reprinted by Skoob Books in 1992. Three years later, a follow up companion—*"The R'lyeh Text"*—appeares, also edited by George Hay, but this time giving more credit to the alleged "researcher" of both books, Robert Turner. To add a dose of credibility, both books include an introduction by Colin Wilson—well known for his prolific writings on the "supernatural" and "occult" topics for many decades.

As a harsh critique of the efforts—representing a focal turning point of energy for misguided ceremonialists, Hay's "*Necronomicon: Book of Dead Names*" (and its companion) do little more than provide Seekers with some less than necessary New Age fluff regarding reinvention of Lovecraft's vision of an ancient paradigm. But we have no need for Lovecraft's semantics of an "alien-god system." We know better—that one actually does exist, extending into the prehistoric consciousness of men—and such is much more worthy of pursuit.

Even as magickal texts go, Hay's "*Necronomicon: Book of Dead Names*" and "*R'lyeh Text*" really do offer quite little (as we are inclined to agree with our predecessors in their critiques). It is more likely that these books were created for personal reasons and originally for a specific network of readers.

The entice in prescribing ceremonial occult attributes to Lovecraft's mythos is furthered in these works by mere mention of more verifiable connections to these arts: Enochian magic of John Dee; references of Lovecraft in Kenneth Grant's work; possible similarities to Crowley's "*Book of the Law*"—all of which, if we are to take the Hay/Turner materials at face value, actually play little or no part in the system of "practical magick" that is even offered in the books. If they are not taken "seriously," and are instead obtained to be a part of some Lovecraftian literary collection, then the two books are intriguing in the light of a fictional "Cthulhu cycle," with a certain nostalgia to them. They will not, however, aid the Seeker in further reaching "*self-honesty*" or unveiling the *Great Deception* that has befallen both the world of light and darkness, alike.

◊ ◊ ◊   ◊ ◊ ◊   ◊ ◊ ◊

The basic *Necronomicon* archetype—an arcane tome divulging esoteric secrets from another time, even before men, when "gods" walked the earth—self-defines its own existence as integral to "*Akashic Records*." These localize on the "*astral plane*"—containing knowledge of the inter-dimensional omniverse.

Aside from Semitic-influenced Gnostic scriptures (such as those found among the *Nag-Hammadi* collections in the mid-twentieth century), the most ancient records mirroring the type of lore we are after, is again, the cuneiform tablets of Mesopotamia—an aspect central to the Simonian and Mardukite interpretation of the *Necronomicon* legacy.

Donald Tyson casually remarks that his inspiration for a Lovecraftian *Necronomicon* cycle came from the astral—and we know that Lovecraft's own inspiration was derived from "dreams of terror and death" and other obscure nightmares—essentially experienced in the astral—so the chances of experienced magicians intentionally tapping these otherworldly forces are actually fairly good. And what's more: the "magician," "priest" or "priestess" is often the bridge—or "*gate*"—inviting these primordial energies to manifest on "*our side*" of the "*Tree.*" Kenneth Grant concurs:—

> "Does this mean that those from Outside will actually put in an appearance on earth? If so, then the secret rites hinted at in grimoires such as the *Necronomicon,* and the *Books of Thoth*, of *Dzyan*, of *Enoch*, contain the keys to their summoning and we have for long aeons been blind to their usage..."

As a perfect example, we find *H. P. Blavatsky's* Theosophical "*Book of Dzyan*" mentioned specifically by Grant—and its even appears as the *Mardukite Tablet-D* series found within "*Necronomicon: The Anunnaki Bible.*"

However, Lovecraftian references specific to the *Necronomicon* are few and far between—in spite of the tremendous attention it has received from his work. There is little to draw from directly in Lovecraft's writings for which to actually base anything other than an *idea*.

Lovecraft did well to keep an aura of mystery shrouding his tome—enough to make people believe it had to exist, but so cryptic as to make it nearly impossible for it to be so. Certainly, no reconstruction (with the exception of the Mardukite *Necrono-*

micon legacy produced by the Mardukite Chamberlains) has ever truly lived up to what the fanatics crave—part of this due to their very attachment to the Lovecraftian mythos: if the *Necronomicon* can be purchased in any store, then it loses the edge of mystery so sacred to its existence. Aliens and gods aside, a person's own "psyche" has the ability (is essentially programmed) to deceive them into playing inconsequential logic games with semantic understanding of basic things—leading nowhere.

Let us consider, then, what options remain now for the Seeker, Adept or Master: *First*—you could go back to a familiar world of forms, embrace the mathematical precision and beauty of the *"Realm of Light"* in all of its worldly glamour, and *take the "blue pill"* as it were—all of this we speak of is pure fantasy and your parents and civil leaders know better; *Second*—you can choose to invite into your life any and all things "opposite" to this realm, thrashing about in your cage, cursing your wardens, demanding to make the "fantasy" real, Lovecraftian or otherwise, because anything is better than the program you continue to subject yourself to; or, *Thirdly*—to extend your mind back to the farthest reaches of space and time to unveil the mysteries of not only what you have been shown, but also what you have not been shown, to drink deeply from the very real source of lore available to those who "initiate" to seek it.

Necronomicons appearing and remaining in the "New Age" usually are based specifically on Lovecraftian literature. Yet, during the 1980's and 90's, several small print run editions of strictly "Simonian" companions emerged—most of which offered very little "new" information to enhance the system. Many rehashes by obsessed fans of the *Schlangekraft recension* started showing up—including *"Hidden Keys of the Necronomicon"* and *"Necronomian Workbook,"* published by a small underground press called I.G.O.S.—"the International Guild of Occult Sciences."

During its short existence, "I.G.O.S." was run by someone named *"Brother Moloch"*—author of the surprisingly expensive (now out-of-print) *"Necronomian Workbook."* He also seems to share Simon's fascination with the *Red Dragon Grimoire*—also known as the *Grand Grimoire*. Avon/HarperCollins briefly republished the grimoire as a "Simon" book, titled "*Papal Magic.*" Its supporting material quite strongly and covertly resembled an existing work by Tracy Twyman—"*The Magic of St. Peter*"—which the same company had previously declined to publish. According to Twyman, she had even asked for Lavenda's assistance in presenting it to Avon.

These types of "grimoire" carry a strong archetypal tradition in older circles—sharing a similar energetic current as the *Necronomicon*. Most modern practitioners and "New Age" readers also seem primarily concerned about ritual magic for material gain. The arrangement of traditional "grimoires" and emphasis on "spells" from "witchcraft" revivals may be the cause—or else, it is just human nature. But, the *Necronomicon* is essentially an archetype of the most ancient beliefs and traditions on the planet —whether in Lovecraft's fantasy or as part of the Mesopotamian cycle—and it therefore has much more to offer than a few "love spells" and "money charms."

The arrival of Simon's *Necronomicon* awoke the consciousness of the global population to forces—very real forces—that had long since been forgotten. This is an essential part of required "Nex-Gen" changes happening on the planet—in brief: the return of the "*Old Ones,*" just as Lovecraft predicted, envisioned, or *dreamed*. Most of us are indoctrinated from birth with familiar parochial and Biblical interpretations of these ancient traditions —but they have not been "realized" clearly for literally thousands of years. Such would, in itself, deem the pursuit worthy enough—but more importantly, with historical validity.

In spite of controversy over the title, Simon's book represents *first steps* toward a true "Mardukite" system. After the official inception of the modern "Mardukite" movement, the *first step* that the Mardukite Chamberlains ("*Mardukite Research Organization*") took in 2009 was to very simply bridge this gap.

The Mardukite "*Liber N—Necronomicon*" was the first discourse prepared, now a part of the greater source book anthology —"*Necronomicon: The Anunnaki Bible.*" It was not intended as a replacement or even competition for the *Schlangekraft recension.*

Instead, it was released to the world as stand-alone volume composed of raw cuneiform tablet materials representing a more complete and verifiable archive—of the *same* sources hidden behind the admittedly bastardized collection of Simon's frugal anthology.

In essence, our Mardukite *Necronomicon* work is intended as a gateway for esoteric Seekers from their more familiar-"unfamiliar" territories, into the much deeper (or "higher") realizations accessible. [Update: these "higher" advancements are now treated as the subject of "Mardukite Systemology" and "Systemology Society.]

THE LADDER OF LIGHTS:
A STAIRWAY TO HEAVEN?

The *Schlangekraft recension* begins with a series of "lessons" dedicated to the sevenfold system of Gates. Mardukite interpretations of the same are referred to as the *Book of Star Gates* or *the Babili Text—Tablet-A* and *Tablet-B* of "*Necronomicon: The Anunnaki Bible*"—drawn from the very heart of Babylon. Attributes, designations and invocation prayers specific to the "younger generation" of *Anunnaki* appearing in the Babylonian system are quite clear. They are also quite verifiable using esoteric archaeology.

For personal experimentation, suitable independently researched substitutions for "Simonian invocations" were easily found by the Mardukite Chamberlains from the *Kuyunjik* cuneiform tablet collection, preserved at the British Museum—fully described in Joshua Free's companion work (to *Liber-R*) found in the *Gates of the Necronomicon* anthology (materials also released as "*The Sumerian Legacy*" or "*Sumerian Religion*" by Joshua Free). This tablet series—called NIS KATI—is more "famously" known in scholarly circles as the *Prayers of the Lifting of the Hand*—or alternately, "*Raising of the Hand.*" Additional work by by the Mardukite Chamberlains resulted in a new standard for modern Anunnaki invocation methods—*The Book of Marduk by Nabu*—included in more recent editions of "*Necronomicon: The Anunnaki Bible*" as the *Tablet-W* series.

Simon's "Banishings and Exorcisms" are reminiscent of "magic" found on the MAKLU (or MAQLU) tablets, and are easily identifiable. He presents his chapter as "The Book of the Burning of Evil Spirits." Many of the incantations are identical to those published scholarly as the "*Maqlu Tablet Series*" ("*The Burnings*").

Simon even includes other various incantations from Akkadian and Assyrian origins—the "*Surpu Tablet Series*" ("*The Consuming*") or the "*Utukku Limnuti Series*" ("*Of Evil Spirits*")—all of which are described in more detail within "Liber-9" [included within this present "*Novem Portis*" reissue] and our Mardukite "*Necronomicon: The Anunnaki Bible.*" More than simply the exorcism of evil spirits, or a manual to anti-demon healing rites—such as is more the case with the other tablet series mentioned here—the *Maqlu Series* targets specifically those who feed "evil" its existence: *the wicked-witch and evil sorcerer.*

Colorfully broadcast across nine cuneiform tablets, the *Maqlu* research conducted by Mardukite Chamberlains in 2011 through 2019 provided *Tablet-M* translations for more recent editions of Mardukite materials, including "*Liber-M*," available as "*The Maqlu Ritual Book*" by Joshua Free, and included in the Master Edition hardcover anthology: "*Necronomicon: The Complete Anunnaki Legacy.*"

Even in its raw untranslated forms, a diligent Seeker or Adept can easily find correlations between the earlier Simon and later Mardukite works. For example, Simon's version illustrates "A Most Excellent Charm Against the Hordes of Demons that Assail in the Night," to be used while censoring the sacred circle with incense, or sprinkling blessed waters, while using the following untranslated incantation:—

ISA YA! ISA YA! RI EGA! EI EGA!
BI ESHA BI ESHA! XIYILQA! XIYLQA!
DUPPIRA ATLAKA ISA YA U RI EGA
LIMNUTTIKUNU KIMA QUTRI LITILLI SHAMI YE
INA ZUMRI YA ISA YA
INA ZUMRI YA RI EGA
INA ZUMRI YA BI ESHA
INA ZUMRI YA XIYILQA
INA ZUMRI YA DUPPIRA
INA ZUMRI YA ATLAKA
INA ZUMRI YA LA TATARA
INA ZUMRI YA LA TETIXXI YE
INA ZUMRI YA LA TAQARRUBA
INA ZUMRI YA LA TASANIQA

NI YISH SHAMMASH KABTU LU TAMATUNU
NI YISH ENKI BEL GIMRI LU TAMATUNU
NI YISH MARDUK MASHMASH ILANI LU TAMATUNU
NI YISH GISHBAR QAMIKUNU LU TAMATUNU
INA ZUMRI YA LU YU TAPPATTASAMA!

Compare this to final incantation from the fifth tablet of *Mardukite Liber-M* (or *Tablet-M*) *"Maqlu Tablet Series"* used for *"The Maqlu Ritual Book"*:—

i-sa-a i-sa-a ri-e-qa ri-e-qa
  Go away! Go away! Be gone! Be gone!
bi-e-šá bi-e-šá hi-il-qa hi-il-qa
  Stay away! Stay away! Flee! Flee!
dup-pi-ra at-la-ka i-sa-a u ri-e-qa
  Get off! Go away! Stay away! Be gone!
limuttu-ku-nu ki-ma qut-ri li-tel-li šamêe
  Your evil spell, like smoke, rises skyward into nothing!
[170] ina zumri-ia i-sa-a
  From my body, keep off!
ina zumri-ia ri-e-qa
  From my body, be gone!
ina zumri-ia bi-e-šá
  From my body, depart!
ina zumri-ia hi-il-qa
  From my body, flee!
ina zumri-ia dup-pi-ra
  From my body, get off!
[175] ina zumri-ia at-la-ka
  From my body, go away!
ina zumri-ia la tatârâ
  From my body, turn away!
ina zumri-ia la tetehêe
  From my body, do not approach!
ina zumri-ia la taqarubâ
  From my body, do not come near!
ina zumri-ia la tasaniqâqa
  From my body, do not touch!
[180] ni-iš SAMAS kabti lu ta-ma-tu-nu
  By the breath of Shammash, Radiant One,

you are commanded!
ni-iš E-A BEL naqbi lu ta-ma-tu-nu
 By the breath of Enki, Lord of the Deep,
 you are commanded!
ni-iš Asariludu maš-maš ilimeš lu ta-ma-tu-nu
 By the breath of Marduk, Magician of the Gods,
 you are commanded!
ni-iš GIRRA qa-mi-ku-nu lu ta-ma-tu-nu
 By the breath of Girra, your Executioner,
 you are commanded!
ina zumri-ia lu-u tap-par-ra-sa-ma
 Indeed, you shall be kept from my body!

The primary body of "spiritual scripture" supporting the tradition in the *Schlangekraft recension* is called the *"Magan Text"*—a version of tablet cycles better known elsewhere as the *"Enuma Elis"* and *"Descent of Inanna."* The specific texts used for Simon's work do not appear elsewhere in scholarly translations, but its elements are the same as those scattered among various tablets from Mesopotamia. This suggests that the *"Magan Text"* is a combination of several epics—which were separated accordingly in the Mardukite *"Necronomicon: The Anunnaki Bible."*

But, it should be understood that the admittedly "bastardized" versions appearing in Simon's work are shorter concise—almost portable—versions of other actual tablets. [Update: the Founding Church of Mardukite Zuism now distributes more complete portable versions of our work, such as *"The Complete Book of Marduk"* and *"Anunnaki Bible: The Cuneiform Scriptures (New Standard Zuist Edition)."*] This even furthers the idea that this *Necronomicon* of a "Mad Arab" was not an original "priest guide" or "Babylonian manual" at all, but a crude attempt to preserve such—perhaps the result of a later underground oral tradition. But, the alleged "Mad Arab" author is wrong on one specific detail about his text:—

"The verses here following come from the secret text of some of the priests of a cult which is all that is left of the Old Faith that existed before Babylon was built..."

This would mean "*Sumerian*," and we know this is wrong because, the "*Magan Text*," in both its Simonian version and the specific cuneiform tablets it is based on, are *not* Sumerian—or pre-Babylonian at all—but is the very composition of epics used by priests and priestesses for religious, spiritual and political propagation of none other than a "Mardukite" Babylon!

A "younger generation" of *Anunnaki* "gods" were elevated to a superior status by the "Nabu-priests" of *Babylon*. The "Mardukite" cuneiform tablets of *Nabu* to *Marduk* were forged in *Babylon*, providing evidence to support *Marduk* as "King of the Gods." This is part of what is hidden beneath the "*Magan Text*" of the *Schlangekraft recension*, as the "Mad Arab" explains:—

> "Remembering is the most important and most potent magic, being the Remembrance of Things Past and the Remembrance of Things to Come, which is the same Memory."

To reiterate: the first part of Simon's "*Magan Text*" is little more than a version of the quite famous and most widely influencing of Babylonian tablets: the *Epic of Creation*—also known as the *Enuma Elis*, and given as *Tablet-N* in "*Necronomicon: The Anunnaki Bible*." The original text may have once developed from an earlier Sumerian paradigm of cosmogenesis, but in this Babylonian version, MARDUK is elevated to "King of the Gods"—a position earned by slaying the primeval ancestral dragon—TIAMAT—in a primordial "*War in Heaven*," thereby putting "cosmic order" in the universe.

Another famous cuneiform series—The *Descent of Ishtar*—also appears within the Mardukite cycle of Babylonian tablets (given as the Mardukite *Tablet-C* series) and Simon's "*Magan Text*," where it is referred to as the "*Sleep of Ishtar*." As politically dramatic as the *Enuma Elis* was for Babylon, the *Descent of Ishtar* provided a "passion play" of spiritual material illustrating the nature of the *Underworld*. Much of the material used in "death cults"—which is to say "*gate cults*"—originates here and even in Egypt, where the "dog-star cult" is dedicated to *Anubis* as the "Guardian of the Death Gates."

When interpreting these cycles, spiritual realizations can be overshadowed by physical geographic descriptions—"descent" and "under"—indicating specific relative direction. Mardukite Tradition realized this more in the sense of inter-spacial transitioning, or more preferably—*crossings!* Similar lore is preserved as the Egyptian "*Book of the Dead*," concerning "gates" and "pylons"—also included as part of the *Tablet-C* cycle in "*Necronomicon: The Anunnaki Bible*" for comparison.

In Simon's *Necronomicon*, a few cryptic passages appear as part of the "*Magan Text*," separating the two primary tablet epics. The materials from Akkadian and Assyrian exorcism tablets, concerning "*Seven Demonic Forces*," sometimes referred to as the MASKIM or MASQIM. Temple healers and priestesses often used the *Masqim* concept to understand and cure physical ailments and emotional issues plaguing the population—driving away, in their perspective, the unfavorable unseen spirits along with the unfavorable physical or visible conditions. We see evidence for this work very clearly in the "*Surpu*" tablet series—discussed in the Mardukite *Tablet-H* series of "Liber-9" (included within this present anthology). The nature of such beings is often represented as morally "evil," but they are a *part* of the cosmos —connected to the Source as active powers of otherwise morally-neutral (or amoral) forces.

"Ethical" polarity of any phenomenon tends to be based on observed physical effects or experiences in one's own reality—a mountain or wasteland region can even become "evil" when it is met as an obstacle to overcome or cross. These impressions (or "emotional imprints") are not "momentary"—they can continue to affect memory and human consciousness long after the original stimulus is withdrawn.

The closing passages of the "*Magan Text*,"—with the exception of including the name "CUTHALU"—may be relatively familiar to many Seekers. They are a version of the very words used in many modern occult operations of ceremonial magic—derived from the "*Chaldean Oracle Tablets*," appearing as the Mardukite *Tablet-O* series in "*Necronomicon: The Anunnaki Bible*."

In the Western World, few outside the realm of academia still use the term "Chaldean." In common consciousness, its mystical tradition is simply absorbed into what we might just readily call *Babylonian* today. "Babylon" was a city and a nation. But, the mystical culture developing within it became known as "Chaldean" during a pinnacle of its Renaissance under King Nebuchadnezzar II. Rooted in observing a celestial *"Arien Age"* of *Marduk*, "Chaldean-magic" is a stellar-oriented (or "astral") system of mysticism focused on "stars" and "planetary forces" far more than earthly and worldly elements.

In the *Schlangekraft recension*, remnants of the ancient Mardukite tradition, once implemented in Babylon, are brought to an accessible level for modern ceremonial magicians previously experienced with medieval "kabbalistic" grimoires of sorcery. For those less experienced, Simon's *"Necronomicon Spellbook"* (originally called the *"Necronomicon Report"*) reached the public in the 1980's, attempting to capitalize on what its editors considered as the "grimoire" portions.

Quite curiously, the main "grimoire" part of the work is an interpretation of the seventh ("secret") tablet from the *"Enuma Elis"*—given within the present catalogue as Mardukite *Tablet-F*. This final tablet of the cycle illustrates how, *after* slaying the dragon TIAMAT and fashioning the heavens and the earth, *Marduk* becomes "King" among the *Anunnaki* gods, taking on the sacred names of the preexisting Anunnaki Assembly—*fifty names* to be precise.

The "Mardukite" magician is instructed to appeal to *Marduk*—or in some respects, one of his *names*—for any and all spiritual and magical requests. This includes pathwork on the *"Ladder of Lights"*—system developed in Babylon for the "younger generation" of Anunnaki gods. If they could be more accessible to the people (then their ancestors) then they would be the favored representative powers ingrained into the reality (consciousness) of the people.

Simon's *Necronomicon* makes frequent mention of the "distant and forgetful nature of the gods," but such could just as equally apply to forgetful and easily misled beliefs of humans that have shared participation in "separating" or "fragmenting" reality by their own existence and thought-forms. Perhaps this is part of the maddening realizations H. P. Lovecraft spoke of regarding acquisition of such "divine knowledge" or "gnosis" from the *Necronomicon,* because at the end of the day, the real demon—*the real devil*—that seems to thwart, restrain, devour and destroy you, is *yourself!*

Many pursuing Simon's *Necronomicon*—or essentially any *Necronomicon*—often seeking a specific type of "ritualized grimoire," and the "Book of Fifty Names" provided that for the reader. It was designed to. What may not be easily discerned is: that work, later recreated as the *"Necronomicon Report,"* was a frugal manufacture by Magickal Childe, and essentially Herman Slater.

Larry Barnes also seems to have been adamant about the Avon printing of the work, published as the *"Necronomicon Spellbook,"* all primarily for financial reasons. This is clearly evident by anyone who has compared the *"Necronomicon Spellbook"* to their original *"Necronomicon."* In some ways, the goal was still fueled by a specific mystical intention—to make the *Necronomicon* mythos that much more accessible to people.

Experienced practitioners of ceremonial magic are usually able to glean most of the rudimentary "practical" aspects of Simon's work without need of a guidebook. Such "guides" become questionably necessary only when the "uninitiated" seek short cuts for uncovering the same mysteries as those who are dedicating their lives to the endeavor in Self-Honesty. These other psuedo-sorcerers have no personal investment in uncovering the *ancient arcanum* and likewise carry no responsibility for it. They rarely even look to the ancient sources themselves and often rely on others to do this busy work for them—equally reliant on interpretation by someone else.

Naturally, these forces cannot be fooled or culled into submission, and the metaphysical application that is so popular is in many ways a self-deception. Systematic traditions, hermetically sealed within themselves, rose from Semitic grimoire-styled "ceremonial magick." They are not surprisingly rooted in more ancient Egypto-Babylonian "Hermetic" forms of ritual magic—first the domain of *Enki*, later passed to the possession of *Marduk*, and then his scribe-son *Nabu*. These three figures appear under different names in various mystical traditions all around the planet, each expressed entirely differently based on language and cultural worldviews.

Personal, individuated and subjective experience certainly colors reality. It is inescapable. The real challenge comes when the written word must be employed to bring something that is truly "occult"—existing only in the shadows of human consciousness—into the *"Realm of Light"* for the people to see. This must be done by the *hand* of someone—no matter how divine the "gospel" may be—and is, in many ways, always limited to their own vocabulary, speech and understanding.

As time passes on, simple truths can become very elaborate mysteries due to the manner in which the knowledge is preserved. If the technology of today is the "magic" of yesterday—might what we see as "aliens" and "monsters" of today, as H. P. Lovecraft suggests, be the *gods of yesterday?* Simon admits in *"Dead Names"* that for his project:—

> "...some mysterious power that has used us
> to midwife itself into consciousness."

This is very much the case—except in this instance, the "mysterious power" is not so mysterious to the initiated. It carries with it a name that is not at all present in any Lovecraftian literature—the name of *Marduk*.

◊ ◊ ◊   ◊ ◊ ◊   ◊ ◊ ◊

Deep analysis of Mesopotamian traditions reveals that ancient priest-magicians and priestesses of Babylon did not necessarily use "magic" of the specific nature described in Simon's work. This type of "grimoire magic" emerged later. At best, ancient Mardukites would invoke powers of the *Anunnaki* using incantations in the name of *Marduk*. This idea of using "secret names" as properties of *Marduk*—or any other demigod—for "spellcraft" and "low magic" is a much more recent addition to the system.

As magical systems evolved, later operators and scions of the traditions were kept in fear—in the "dark"—concerning the true nature of cosmic power, the Anunnaki, and structure of material reality as a whole.

After the "gods" left the earth, what they left behind was designed so that those who might "stumble upon" the secrets of the gods would not understand what they behold. Instead, they would be lost to lifetimes of "mystifying correspondences" and numerological calculations—but never finding the way out! There are others locked in the matrix-web of material reality— those who do not succumb to the "occult" enlightenment trappings—who feel they are *above* such "superstition," the physical sciences were devised for the Realm of Light—simply another self-validating semantic paradigm used to base reality. The need to "know" and "label" creates new semantics to "know about." Yet, the "whole" is still unchanged.

The true cosmic nature of all things is much more "basic" than these systems provide understanding for.True knowledge remains simultaneously "hidden" and "in front of" all humanity. But the human psyche sees it, not for what it is, but refracted in a world of lights. People are naturally conditioned to remain enamored with the spectrum of variegated colors dancing on the wall rather then the unifying source of them. Mystical and "magickal work" is no different than other physical sciences provide.

Modern "ritual magick" techniques are based on the same work conducted by the ancient *"Nabu-Tutu"* cults of Babylon—and later Egypt—but they concealed mysteries exclusive to their own inner circles, of a more "spiritual" nature—a more direct means to the Source without the trappings of the system.

Evidently, the ancient Mardukite Babylonians distinguished between their "esoteric" or secret knowledge and the "exoteric" or public display of knowledge intended for the masses. The public tablets, literature and traditions were raised to preserve a secret spiritual system—reserved for those "who know"—a secret "illuminated" class of society. This is alluded to in many "mystery traditions" and "mystic schools" throughout history— and yet they, themselves, have not been able to overcome glamours inherent in the human condition.

Both mainstream and niche religions are no different, but unfortunately those who find this out are often so overcome with despair that they fall victims to any alternate fantasy or succumb to lifestyles rooted in hedonistic delights—"stooping down into a darkly splendid world." They fall prey to a atheistic and nihilistic "*Its all crap*" mentalities, having nothing of substance to fill the void. Consider the words of the "*Chaldean Oracles*" rendered as the *Tablet-O* series in "*Necronomicon: The Anunnaki Bible*":—

> *Do not fix your mind on the vast systems of the Earth;*
> *For the Plant of Truth grows not upon the ground.*
> *Move, therefore, away from the Material World,*
> *If you should enter the Star-Gate of the Sacred Paradise,*
> *Where only Virtue, Wisdom and Unity are assembled.*
> *Stoop not, therefore, down unto this Darkly-Splendid World;*
> *Wherein lies a continually faithless depth,*
> *And Hades shrouded in cloudy gloom,*
> *Delighting in senseless images...*

The forces "sealed" into currents of the magician's craft are the same "*Gates*" or "*veils*" of existence found in Anunnaki literature —called "*zonei*" in Simonian material. These forces describe a band of "seven lights" composing the spectrum of "form" that we experience as the "Material World."

These "vibrations"—forces in motion—are the "*Cosmic Laws*" of the systematic universe as it was "designed." They really have no names or attributes themselves, except as we ascribe when communicating an understanding of them. At this point, the experienced practitioner can learn to be a master of the rays or allow them to be his or her master. This is not only a decision or feat of willpower—it requires an entire restructuring of the psyche. Do you serve the "deception" or become a Master ("Ascended"?) of the Spheres—rightfully taking your place among the "gods" outside of this material existence—"*and in the spaces between...*"

◊ ◊ ◊   ◊ ◊ ◊   ◊ ◊ ◊

Before the 31st Anniversary resurgence of the Simon hardcover, Avon (HarperCollins) published mass-market paperback editions of the new "Simon" books in 2006. Simon's version of "*Gates of the Necronomicon*" discourse reached the public on Samhain that year, six months after a Beltane appearance of "*Dead Names: The Dark History of the Necronomicon.*" These two critical "gate threshold" periods were chosen intentionally, coinciding with this "magical tradition." Simultaneously, 2006 was the same year work began to solidify the inception of the modern "Mardukite" movement led by Joshua Free—a vision realized publicly (online) two years later in 2008.

Renewed interest in this paradigm followed the release of Simon's "*Gates*" material, helping to pave the way for a new millennium phase-shift of Mardukite revival. Emphasis returns to Egyptian and specifically Mesopotamian influences on the system—particularly the sevenfold *stargate* paradigm. As we discover, all of this is critically connected to the "magick" of this world—specifically the very manner in which the world itself operates by design. But, one of the most reoccurring key symbolic elements in esoteric lore is the connection made between "*gates*" and "*stars.*"

The fundamental principles or laws of the cosmos—forces of "gods," "stars" and "planets"—eventually blended together in human consciousness; just as the aspects of "god," "sky" and "heaven" were all represented by a single Sumerian character —"AN." Any distinction in understanding between these natures is lost to language and human over-identification of knowledge with strictly "words" and "labels."

In a methodology of reality separated into "levels" of existence, these "gates" represent the pathways, avenues or bridges of communication and power "between the veils." Beyond these *veils*, all of existence experiences its own entangled and unified nature with the ALL. The true magician does not succumb to an "illusion of power," falsely believing himself a god from pride, but instead realizes that it is the ability to communicate and facilitate communication with the "fabric of space" that causes manifestation—by the powers of the "God-Source!" This is what has been concealed in the dark and and "shadowy" side of the occult—for the more self-deluded that "magicians" and "dabblers" become in their own conceptions of enlightenment, the less likely they are to see the forest for the trees—and the deeper the enslavement to their own systems.

Representations of a "Celestial Gate"—to "outside" of the system —are mythographically transposed onto the "Celestial Pole." By definition, this is the planet's "naturally ordained" axial relationship with the "Celestial Sphere"—an astronomical term used to define the zodiacal band of stars visible when we look relatively "out" into the universe, significant to the "precession" or relative movement of bodies in this solar system. In the most ancient recorded times of Mesopotamia, the central polar starbody or "constellation" was the "Dragon"—*Draco*—particularly the star *Thuban*. As of several thousand years ago, the "Great Bear" took dominance as the "Time Keeper of the Heavens," revolving around the star *Polaris*. A shift from centralization of the Dragon to the Bear reflected in cultural interpretations of traditions and lore evolving from earlier, more ancient eras.

> *The Dragon was defeated!*
> *It lay below now, "dead but dreaming,"*
> *overtaken by the Bear!*

The fierce bear-king in Egypto-Babylonian traditions became "MARDUK-RA"—but this was only "truth" to the *"younger generation"* of *Anunnaki* "gods" of Babylon—their perception; their story. The primordial "Ancient Ones" predating the more familiar Mardukite Babylonian pantheon were once honored by a much more ancient "Dragon-cult"—dedicated to the ancient primeval cosmic serpent mother of life—TIAMAT.

Simonian discourses unknowingly [we assume] continue to perpetuate the same deception of polarity raised by the "younger," who gave themselves the name "Elder Gods" in order to secure a further separation of their divine nature from their ancestors of antiquity. Unfortunately, even in the 2006 edition of Simon's "*Gates of the Necronomicon*," *Marduk* is still referred to as a "*Sumerian*" god—which is not really the case.

We find the same misnomer quite often in Zecharia Sitchin's work as well. *Marduk* existed, but he was never recognized officially in the pre-Babylonian *Sumerian* "pantheon"—a detail that may seem trite to some, but as the modern Mardukites discovered in discerning the origins of their own organization—it is actually quite significant.

As a general classification, the term "Mesopotamian" is quite preferable when the exact nature is not always readily available. This encompasses not only the prehistoric *Ubaid* and *Sumerians*, but also the later emerging *Babylonian* (*Chaldean*), *Akkadian*, *Assyrian* (*&tc.*) cultures that all shared similar languages, religion and geography—their interpretations of the mysteries merely separated with time, shifting in the sands of the desert "between two rivers."

The *Schlangekraft recension* also refers to the "*Anunnaki*" as separate from the system or else as the "Seven Judges of the Underworld." Early works by Sumeriologist, Samuel N. Kramer, often related them as "*Earth gods.*" The IGIGI are portrayed as a race of demon-Watchers, somehow separate from the class of "Guardian Watcher Spirit"—or "*sedu*"—conjured to a magicians side for each ritual observation from that grimoire.

Simon's research into the "Celestial Gate" is intriguing. He suggests that the "Great Bear" constellation is the "astral key" that activates the *Gate* from the earth perspective, when the *bear* "hangs from its tail." How curious—this actually happens every day! But, it is not only the event itself, but the timing or threshold that is significant—it is when the remaining "stars are aligned" that the *Gate* is functional *from our side*.

Where much has been written elsewhere concerning Samhain—October 31—when this "Celestial Gate" is most accessible *from the other side*, it is really at the other half of the year, at Beltane—April 30—when this alignment happens shortly before midnight, a natural ceremonial time for such mystical work. If this is correct, it suggests a convergence in "earth-time" with "heaven-time." Ceremonial execution would then require a delicate calculation of sun-cycles, lunar-cycles and stellar-cycles.

So, now the seeker must put the "gate-theory" into perspective. Not only is it something that happens "naturally" on a daily basis, it is observed (and apparently ceremonially effective) only under the most opportune times, and then too, subject to a calculation that might be mistaken. Where then, does the fear come from for "leaving this gate open for too long"...?

THE INFLUENCE OF
H.P. LOVECRAFT

Contributions of H.P. Lovecraft—and the *"Cthulhu Mythos"*—are mostly absent from earliest work of the modern "Mardukites"—particularly *"Necronomicon: The Anunnaki Bible."* His contributions play a very passive role in our researches—which mainly emphasize, specifically, the "Anunnaki" and "Mesopotamian" aspects of the legacy.

The questions of *sanity* and *reality* are the two primary themes prevalent in all of Lovecraft's work. It is not surprising that "Simon" begins his *"Gates of the Necronomicon"* discourse with a semantic lesson on these two words. According to H. P. Lovecraft's existential perceptions, arcane knowledge is very dangerous when we factor in the human element. So long as the characters accept what they have been given as the "norm" of society (via social conditioning) there is no question of sanity—reality is one-to-one with the consensus of the Realm. But what if this were not the case? What if things are only "real" from a matter of perspective—a deeper truth veiling the way things are as an Absolute? Or, perhaps there are no absolutes—this would also be a very "maddening" realization as well: *things are only the way they are because that is how we see them.*

Forces exist in the universe—active principles of "Cosmic Law" in perpetual motion. They are actually quite amoral—without mundane morality—and exist solely to feed the operation of "existence" as it is. The material world is fashioned to function as necessity. The way in which this is subjectively perceived has little to do with the fact that it must function, and continues to function *with or without* our agreement. Of course, a systematically fractured universe requires a degree of intricacy to keep in order. Polarized forces seem set against each other to keep the program active. But, they are opposite only in their outer natures—as they are perceived. But in truth—they are the same —two sides of the same degree. That the human mind wishes to fragment some as "good" and others "bad" becomes its own device—its own way from which to view the world.

H. P. Lovecraft's "*Cthulhu Mythos*" is therefore not reality as it is, but reality as some humans have come to interpret their experiences. We are simply given a glimpse of one man's fragmented experience of universal forces and how they relate to one another. Quoting fantasy role-playing game developer, *Monte Cook:—*

> "These forces taken together are not the Cthulhu Mythos, however. They are simply reality, the way things are. The body of knowledge known as the Cthulhu Mythos is the result of human attempts to make sense of this reality. We interact with these forces in tentative ways, and come away with suspicions about their true nature. Like medieval physicians who believed that stomach aches were caused by a small imp lodged in the belly, we look into the night sky and think we know what's there. We're wrong, because we can never truly know the darkness."

H.P. Lovecraft's personal experiences, visions and meditations interacting with these primordial forces manifested in his literary work—always presented as works of fiction—keeping any esoteric meaning enshrouded in mystery. Regardless of whether or not he researched lore of Dogon tribes in Africa, or Oannes myths of Mesopotamia, or if his family had involvement with Egyptian Freemasonry—Lovecraft was plagued by his own very real dreams and nightmares of terror and occult horror— and they do not seem to have subsided in his waking reality.

From his own subjective perceptions, "Lovecraft's Universe" was essentially *bad.* Color this however poetically with "*black seas of infinity*" and other word pictures—essentially, from the viewpoint of humanity, bad things happen for no reason, or bad things happen causally from human actions (such as opening the mind to the *Necronomicon* or opening some other gateway), but ultimately in the end—*bad things happen.*

◊ ◊ ◊   ◊ ◊ ◊   ◊ ◊ ◊

Nihilism grows like a tumor on Lovecraft's psyche the further he delves into the nature of his visions for the sake of his readers—or, perhaps as a personal coping mechanism. His perspective is very clear though—celebration of the Old Ones is bad; celebration of the new religions is bad; pursuit of the spiritual is bad; materialistic hedonism is bad... and when you factor in all the rest we might add to this, the end result is always the question: *why are we even here?!?* Given this sentiment or any systematic realization of this, the very idea that Lovecraft's characters seek to use the *Necronomicon* to "live forever" or "bring discarnates back" to this wretched existence is clearly *insanity!!!*

By the end of Lovecraft's literary career, scattered details of the *Necronomicon* reached such epic proportions that it seemed that it would be nearly impossible for it to exist. Certainly, no edition in print has ever truly satisfied the strictest of Lovecraftians. And many show they are misguided. The modern "Mardukite Office" was plagued with correspondence following the public release of its "*Liber N—Necronomicon*" in 2009, from those seeking advice on how they might devise and publish their own "beefed up" versions of the legendary tome. We had literally run out of politically correct ways of saying: *you've missed the point, guys.*

Just as is described in stories of Lovecraftian literature, partaking in a real intellectual pursuit of the *Cthulhu Mythos* and *Necronomicon* can become the most dangerous drug available for this existence—a truly unsatisfiable thirst for knowledge. For those who have dismissed the worldly systems of glamour and illusion, there is the deception of enlightenment embedded within the "occult"—another system so convoluted that it keeps the psyche ever perpetually occupied on the unresolvable "mystery" fabricated on the screen.

H. P. Lovecraft never truly designated a specific pantheon for the Old Ones. This was a task left to his interpreters—a task taken up by many in realms of both literary fantasy and practical mysticism.

From the plethora of scattered references composing the "*Cthulhu Mythos*," Robert Turner singled out six specific forces for a version of the pantheon provided in his "*Necronomicon: Book of Dead Names*"—Azathoth, Yog-Sothoth, Nyarlathotep, Hastur, Cthulhu and Shub-Niggurath. In spite of the name adopted for the system, Turner ranks his pantheon in order of presidency, putting Cthulhu somewhere towards the end. Even in these revived Lovecraftian occult traditions, Cthulhu does not take a central role.

Many esoteric mysteries beyond our understanding of "Cosmic Law" bare no readily discernible answers for a fractured human psyche—but, nonetheless the quest ensues, and humans are left to fight amongst themselves with multifaceted interpretations. The lure of H. P. Lovecraft's *Necronomicon* is: just one more moment of power; just one more incantation; just one more deciphered word—will grant the Seeker a key out of the system —the "*Key to the Outside*." And this type of "gambler's fallacy" runs rampant in most "New Age" traditions.

A quick consolidation of Lovecraftian lore combined with Simonian and Mardukite "*Gate*" research and lore, all point toward the threshold time taking place during the ancient annual "*Beltane*" festival. Popularized by the Celts and Druids, there does appear to be some "otherworldly" significance with May's Eve. Lovecraft explains that the time is optimal for receiving primordial knowledge via the "*whisperer in darkness*"—strangely echoing the ceremonial magician's "*voice in the silence*," alluded to in various transcendental occult materials. Lovecraft writes in his prose of the same name, "*The Whisperer in Darkness*":—

> "Former experience had told him May Eve—the hideous Sabbat night of underground European legend—would probably be more fruitful than any other date, and he was not disappointed..."

Even the *Necronomicon* of Lovecraft's visions, however, seem to thwart the Seeker from unveiling the true nature of these beings. As a literary work in itself, Lovecraft's *Necronomicon*—however enlightened or inspired the text may be—was still subject to the same individuated subjective consciousness of its allegedly Arabic author—given as "*Abdul Alhazred.*"

One must wonder about the early experiences of the human populations when encountering physical forces of their "alien gods." Consider the story of Ezekiel's Chariot or even the "burning bush." Previously, mention was made in the introductory materials of "*Necronomicon: The Anunnaki Bible*" concerning the "three angels" who approach Abraham in the deserts... The list is endless. Lovecraft explicitly explains, in his discourse on horror fiction, that it is the "fear of the unknown," above all other human emotions, that is not only traumatic and mentally shocking, but powerful and strong. Fear is unique above the rest—immediately able to bring its bearer to the most primitive base animal reactive levels of survival—*fight or flight!*

Lovecraft's pantheon of gods appear to do little to soothe any human fear—and they use it to their benefit—cloaking themselves in obscure anonymity until the "stars are right" for their return. Will they even return? Did they ever truly leave?

> "It seems that the evil legends about what they have offered to men, and what they wish in connection with the earth, are wholly the result of an ignorant misconception of allegorical speech—how totally we had misjudged and misinterpreted the purpose of the Outer Ones in maintaining their secret colony on this planet..." —*The Whisperer in Darkness*

After spending several decades relaying his gothic horror fantasy encounters with the "*Other*," we receive no apologies—but merely a subtle "oops!" for our efforts in following his previously relayed cycle. Surely, Lovecraftians and academicians alike will point out that such is being taken out of context—from a work of "fiction."

But thematic plot-lines in Lovecraft's cycles are actually quite sparse. It becomes quickly evident that this literature is not meant to relay some horror adventure epic stories—rather, they describe a loosely collected set of ideas and philosophies. Any other background information simply offers a setting to present the lore as "facts"—much as how we might glean our knowledge from history books or newspaper articles.

◊ ◊ ◊   ◊ ◊ ◊   ◊ ◊ ◊

H.P. Lovecraft once explained to his beneficiary. *August Derleth* —"I have something to say, but can't say it..." And it is at this moment that the horror really hits us, for we now know for certain that Lovecraft knows well more than he is letting on. We have experienced it before—because his prolific writings, as insightful as they might be, continue to only be written by the truth of Lovecraft's own experiences—veiled from the reader's casual experiences concerning the "stories" themselves. "The books you read are safe," we remember the bookseller telling Bastian in *The Neverending Story*—"This book is *not* for you."

To better understand the levels of Lovecraft's own realizations of the universe, one might distinguish from what "cycle" of life and literature he writes from. Nearly all of the stories branded as "Cthulhu Mythos" appear towards the end of his lifetime, and yet we see this was not about new conceptions, but simply newer realizations of the same encompassing world.

There were originally no direct efforts made to compile a "pantheon" and Lovecraft never once used the phrase "*Cthulhu Mythos*" to refer to his own work. This a term was later coined by August Derleth. Lovecraft acknowledges that his interpretation is a primitive understanding at best, shaped by the fears of men—part of the evolution in human understanding of what has been hidden—resting in the shadows of mysterious occult esoterica—for thousands of years.

> But let us be clear: *His work is not a stopping point—and those who treat it at such will inevitably realize the "dead end" embedded at the "height" of the system—where no true transcendental experience will be found.*

As described by some esoteric and occult authors, the mind-shattering mysteries of the *Abyss* are tapped during "sexual" experiences. In fact, according to many modern "magickal orders"—usually those involved with or influenced by the work of *Aleister Crowley*—a sexual medium (on some level) is actually required for human consciousness to access any of the "*Gates*."

It is interesting to note that Lovecraft's own "*Cthulhu*" cycle of works begin to emerge during the time he is married (1924-1929). *Kenneth Grant* draws from Rabbinical lore in "*Outer Gateways*," explaining that Moses failed to access these mysteries— the "*Fiftieth*" or "*Final Gate*" (of "*supernal light*") of the cosmos —"because he ceased to live with his wife." Other schools warn students against use of (physical) "sexual magic"—often due to its tendency for abuse, or else to seek "heightened states" through abstinence.

That humanity has been separated from the Source and fractured into individual existences has already been suggested, but in the face of sexual union we experience an even further separation from each other—the very idea of a "union" for mortals denotes a separation in the first place—that parts once divided are rejoined. Complex lust programs deeply ingrained in human consciousness, force the true nature of even *this* to remain veiled.

THE CYCLES OF LOVECRAFTIAN LITERATURE

Macabre – 1905 thru 1920
Dreams – 1920 thru 1927
Cthulhu – 1925 thru 1935

"Now I regret the harm I have inflicted upon these alien and incredible beings in the course of our nightly skirmishes. If only I had consented to talk peacefully and reasonably with them in the first place... But they bear me no grudge, their emotions being organized differently from ours..." —*The Whisperer in Darkness*

This is what causes the distortions in reality—*fear* of the unknown. Just as equally dangerous is the fear of what *can not* be known—or perhaps for some, what *should not* be known. Such thinking turns truth into anathema—just as the fear-program was designed to!

> "All that the Outer Ones wish of man is peace and non-molestation and an increasing intellectual rapport. This latter is absolutely necessary now that our inventions and devices are expanding our knowledge and motions, and making it more and more impossible for the Outer Ones' necessary outposts to exist *secretly* on this planet. The very idea of any attempt to *enslave* or *degrade* mankind is ridiculous." —*The Whisperer in Darkness*

Given that "our eyes have deceived us before," it is rather difficult for a serious student to draw any clear logical conclusion about the nature of "alien gods" solely from Lovecraft's work. Can we be certain this time that these forces are indeed "favorable spirits" as opposed to some other gruesome horrors that have haunted us in the night? Are the ones that created us, going to be the same ones returning? Can we be certain that all forces presenting themselves as "peaceful" actually be the "kindly guardians" of the cosmos we seek? Is there any hope in illuminating the darkness so fixed by the human psyche?

THE CTHULHU CULT

The concept of H. P. Lovecraft's *Necronomicon* became insepar-able from what literary fans and contributors later coined as the "*Cthulhu Mythos*." This collections of writings were never really intended as a functional "pantheon" in itself—but existed as a *cycle* composing the final works of Lovecraft during his lifetime.

Cthulhu makes his first appearance in 1925—a year after Love-craft's marriage. In this new cycle of material, he sought a more definitive form to the thoughts, dreams and visions haunting his life. He sought to understand the causal universal reality as it had affected him—as his personal experience dictated it him and how he in turn communicated to his readers. This *cycle* of "Cthulhu" literature was just as sporadic and sparse as his earli-er works—but then one must remember that these writings were first published as short serials in a magazine called "*Weird Tales*," and very few of them are book-length as stand alone works.

"*Call of Cthulhu*" is a short story debuting the figure now popular among enthusiasts and a familiar name among left-hand-path practitioners, which is to say those who prefer "darker" and more "rebellious" aspects of the occult. One really is led to won-der what "enlightenment" is intended through blatant disregard for natural order—or, the love of chaos. Nonetheless, it is the darker aspects of this "mythos" that attracts attention from the alternative-types, punks and outcasts. Perhaps a "fluf-fier" book on self-help candle meditation methods using flowery imagery, incense and fairy-infused bath soaps has an appeal to lonely witch-type housewives—but, for those seeking more ant-agonistic approaches to "rebelling" against the "reality deception," well, the system always provides, dictating—*Whatever the thinker, thinks; the prover, proves.*

H. P. Lovecraft's *"Call of Cthulhu"* is written as like a "detective mystery," where the rites and activities of a very modern and active "Cthulhu Cult" are described. While the essence of esoteric lore and occult mystery runs deep beneath the surface, just as with any other well-established "cult" in history, the means of enlightenment by quasi-hippie methods of free love, drunken orgies and the like, certainly leave much to be desired —though many *do desire* this method for purely hedonistic ideals, even if they prefer to shroud their beliefs and actions with the illusion of enlightenment.

Celebration of the *lower* is hardly a means to the *higher*. And those mistaking or misusing the secret power embedded intentionally in the *"Sex Gate"* will find the experience to be just as physically, emotionally and spiritually disturbing and damaging as any of the other *"Gates"* method. This is not to say there is not some validity to the methods.

But, the human psyche seems to muddle its experience of "sexual" energies, and so it is not a preferred method of instruction— at least certainly not at any "neophyte" levels of occult initiation. [We might speak the same warnings regarding what some refer to as "psychedelic shamanism."] An initiate must be in a state of absolute "clear" *Self-Honesty*, or the experience will yield yet another pitfall—leaving the Seeker confused, lost—and again, far from true enlightenment.

What can we say for the Humans and their "condition"? They were programmed to enjoy fucking so they wouldn't confuse it with killing—and the emotional charge to make rational sense of both. If sex didn't feel good, for at the very least "evolutionary" purposes, the human race would have bred itself out into extinction a long time ago; programmed for game-condition competition that keeps us from working together and even helping one another. We watch as the race has grown to hate its own, itself and everything "apart" from itself. How dismal, indeed. Perhaps Lovecraft had a point or two after all—when even I have seen inside the human psyche at your best and at your worst and I can usually never tell the difference... Lovecraft writes in *"Call of Cthulhu"*:—

"The most merciful thing in the world, I think, is the inability of the human mind to correlate all it contains. We live on a placid island of ignorance in the midst of black seas of infinity, and it was not meant that we should voyage far. The sciences, each straining in its own direction, have hitherto harmed us little; but some day the piercing together of dissociated knowledge will open up such terrifying vistas of reality, and our frightful position therein, that we shall either go mad from the revelation or flee from the deadly light into the peace and safety of a new dark age."

One way in which the occultists have always dealt with the "maddening revelations" is, again, utter immortality. Although the current editor was mentored at an early age in the methods of the *Hermetic Order of the Golden Dawn* and is aware of the work related to the seemingly "darker" derivatives of the same: *Argentium Astrum* (A.A.) and *Ordo Templi Orientis* (O.T.O.), these have not been the glasses worn from which to envision the modern Mardukite movement, even considering the *Necronomicon* amidst all of the "gore" and "horror" surrounding it.

In the past, many underground "cults" and groups often coped with these "maddening revelations" using some kind of ritual drama or other intentional reenactments intended to trigger states of consciousness—including activities designed to bridge a fiction ("Cthulhu Cult") to history. Among some real groups, especially those influenced directly by Aleister Crowley, these are not unique. For example, similar secret cult rituals were written for *Argentium Astrum* in 1910, known as the *"Rites of Eleusis."*

The *"Rites of Eleusis"* are a perfect example of this celebration of the *lower*—now esoterically relayed to initiates as "religious ecstasy"—to awaken their *higher* faculties. [*Indeed...*] What is not as well known is that there are actually *seven* "Rites of Eleusis"— each corresponds to none other than one of the seven "Zonei" of the *Schlangekraft recension*, or seven "Gates" from the *Babili Texts* in *"Necronomicon: The Anunnaki Bible."*

The "Rites" are presented with the planetary precession we should expect—the precise *Gate* chronology we are already familiar with—*only reversed*. [The order indicated by the "*Rites of Eleusis*" is the "*Ladder of Lights*" in reverse, descending—Saturn, Jupiter, Mars, Sun (Sol), Venus, Mercury and Moon (Luna).] It seems to "key in" sensory entrapment into a physical experience, rather than liberate one from the same.

Participation in such an underground "cult" is very compelling to a certain type of individual. These "inquisitive ones" often venture as deep as they can to unveil what they already know to be a Great Deception. But where is the horizon? Where does the land and sky divide itself—the "real" from the "unreal" ...where? The answer is very clear—it does not. The division is really only within one's own mind—as is the "manifold nature" of reality—as are all the fragmented "*gates*" and "*levels*" that one perceives to exist. The "real" is broadcast all around us—but at an individual level, we can still fail to recognize it for what it is. For this reason, all of the applicable practices and traditions emphasize—*piercing the veils of illusion*.

Why always "underground"—in secret—or with friends? An individual who "stops accepting the program" is semantically "*insane*." When your reality is no longer one-to-one with that which has been given to you, society no longer deems you of a "clean" sound mind. You have gone against the norm—You have broken the veils. Your world reality is now a minority-of-one... Enter: "underground clubs," "secret societies" and "fraternities" that jump at the opportunity to bring the energy and power of another mind under their own group consciousness umbrella of enlightenment. This is yet another layer of glamour embedded into the system for those who "break free." As soon as one "level" is completed—like a game—the next immediately begins and so they must work their way through one labyrinth after another of initiation and indoctrination. This is not the path that all choose, but it is an easy one to succumb to. In a nutshell —if the individual Seeker is, again, not approaching their pursuit in *Self-Honesty*, the result is very likely "getting lost" in yet another system.

Where we might expect details of dismal cult abuse and ab-horred bloody rites, the real intriguing parts of Lovecraft's "Cthulhu cycle"—concerning the "*Old Ones*"—regards classifica-tion of two important details: where they came from and why they were here. Here, described from "*The Whisperer in Dark-ness*"—

> "The Winged Ones came from the Great Bear in the sky, and had mines in our earthly hills whence they took a kind of stone they could not get on any other world. They did not *live* here, but merely maintained outposts and flew back with vast cargoes of stone to their own stars in the north."

This passage, written in the late 1920's or possibly 1930, reveals an emphasis on an area of space that some Seekers are probably all too familiar with—the "*Great Bear*" in the north—but also the mining operations, which we assume to be gold—something we are to expect based on many interpretations of ancient Meso-potamian "Anunnaki" lore. We can consider the context and call it "fiction." But artists and visionaries often choose this method to communicate very real ideas—just like the messages that L. Ron Hubbard received that he described to people in nov-els—such as "*Battlefield Earth*." We should not be so easily dismissive of "fiction" medias by their "fantastical" nature alone. As instructional tools, "stories" and "fables" are timeless methods of communication.

Certainly, many of the original *dystopian* cult classics—*1984*, *Animal Farm*, *Anthem*, *The Giver*—or newer depictions like *Ferngully*, *Avatar*, or even *The Hunger Games*—are all intended to relay very real statements about the world, observations that are more easily communicated *en masse* via the realm of fiction. So long as the end result is a highly marketable work that we can safely store in our mind as a "nice story," we are never truly faced with the total implications of what the artist meant. But the messages are there and they are loud and clear—it is no covert conspiracy. But if they were to really all hit you at once—you might overload! Hence, for good reason, the program keeps people only about 10% conscious of what is happening around them—and this seems sufficient for operating in material existence. This is the most the human condition is designed to handle without self-honesty— think of it as a cosmic "loss prevention" program. Until you can *afford* it, you don't get to have more.

◊ ◊ ◊   ◊ ◊ ◊   ◊ ◊ ◊

"They worshiped, so they said, the Great Old Ones who lived ages before there were any men, and who came to the young world out of the sky. These Old Ones were gone now, inside the earth and under the sea; but their dead bodies had told their secrets in dreams to the first man, who formed a cult which had never died. This was that cult—it had always existed and always would exist, hidden in distant wastes and dark places all over the world until the time when the great priest Cthulhu, from his dark house in the mighty city of R'lyeh under the waters, should rise and bring the earth again beneath his sway. Some day he would call, when the stars were ready, and the secret cult would always be waiting to liberate him."
—*The Call of Cthulhu*

And so, by the act of simply writing this passage, H.P. Lovecraft opened a gate that could allow all these things to manifest in human consciousness—from a certain point of view. It is not necessarily his specific set of semantics (or "*Cthulhu Mythos*") that we need focus attention on—although many do, claiming to have some deep spiritual relationships with "*egregores*"—artificially created thought-form elementaries—manifested from Lovecraft's psyche onto the printed page. [Which is, of course, possible—*from a certain point of view.*] The iconic image of an ancient cult carrying prehistoric knowledge extending to a time before humans could be enough to entice even the most "right wing" Seekers.

To a still sleeping 1920's and 1930's American society, any effective information relay required an acceptable format for public reception. The realm of fantasy and science fiction offers such creative visionary minds an appropriate avenue for expression. Consider the stories of Jules Verne's machines—thought entirely "fanciful" at their time of origination, but they later served as inspiration for technologies. Accounts of the "supernatural" are no different, but rather than use a set framework, paradigm, or systematic vocabulary, the "supernatural" is relayed in Lovecraft's work as the "*Unknown*," something horrific for no other reason than for being the *Unknown*.

When visions turn to gruesome nightmares—and creatures that do not fit within the social norm "one-to-one"—the only way many can interpret them is simply as "monsters." But as Lovecraft began to explain in his final works—"the monsters of today are the gods of yesterday"—and all human communications and relationships with these forces are affected by one's "experiences" and "beliefs." These beliefs or personal determinations define what these experiences implicate on a subjective level.

During initial investigations by the *Mardukite Research Organization*, it seemed many contemporaries and colleagues of the current editor expressed a firm belief that origins of H.P. Lovecraft's "Cthulhu Cult"—and its patron deity, of course—are derived from ancient Middle Eastern lore, but not "Arabic," in the way we understand the region today.

Much like other Chaldeo-Babylonian influences on the modern *Necronomicon* cycle, the Cthulhu archetype does share some proximity with certain ancient currents—but, the relation of it, as demonstrated by Lovecraft's bipolar attitude toward the nature of these beings, is painted over with spiritual politics from a post-Sumerian age. To those already familiar with Mesopotamian mysteries, the name "*Oannes*" is asserted, called "*Dagon*" to Semitic Philistines, as the "truest" identity of Cthulhu—and from this suggestion, we can trace the energy current back to the Anunnaki god, ENKI. When one considers the degradation of the "dragon current"—described in Mardukite *Liber-50* (reissued in paperback as "Sumerian Legacy" by Joshua Free and then in the 2021 hardcover edition "Sumerian Religion")—it is not surprising to see ENKI painted as *a* "Cthulhu" to awakening minds of the 20th century—*many thousands of years after the fact.*

In c. 300 B.C., *Berosus,* a Babylonian historian, left records describing a divine being—amphibian like in nature—named *Oannes.* According to the account, this being emerged in prehistoric times from the Persian Gulf and essentially instructed mankind in the "Divine" arts and sciences of civilization. Then, he disappeared again, back into the sea—*dead but dreaming*—and the people awaited his return.

This concept of a "return" seems fundamental to all religions—that at some indeterminable point in time, an "ultimate confirmation" of one's faith will manifest in front of the whole world. While this definitely assists in sealing systems in consciousness, it is interesting to note that these "messianic" programs are apparently designed to where they always seem to "be coming," but are essentially unfulfillable prophecies in man's eyes. Consider the appearance of Jesus Christ among the Jews—"certainly this cannot be he that the prophets speak of..."

...Do you still deny me?

The lure of the *Cthulhu Cult*—or any similar "cult" following—is essentially the promise of a communion with the "*Other.*" We all know its there—that this isn't all there is—even atheistic minds among you (preferring the semantic taunts of science to religion) still remain amazed about how many apparent "levels" there are to this "physical existence," and the untold secret power that is sealed away therein. That there was something "before" our modern civilization remains beyond the scope of popular public opinions and false ego-centric worldviews.

Humans tend to forget that it was "*to the gods*" that the original esoteric technologies and architecture of the ancient world were first dedicated—not as accomplishments to praise the glory of human labor, such as we might see today. Attributing this ancient knowledge and technology—including the very arts of civilization—to a source other than human is practically mind-shattering to anyone completely closed off to such a "reality."

◊ ◊ ◊   ◊ ◊ ◊   ◊ ◊ ◊

Distinction between the "*Ancient Ones*" (or "*Great Old Ones*") and the younger "*Elder Gods*" has been a matter of confusion for some time. The entire subject was only briefly alluded to in Lovecraft's work. The theme is more commonly related to the *Schlangekraft recension.*

But, as explained in Mardukite *Liber-51/52*, this political and spiritual division really emerged in later interpretations. Complexities of the global system grew from their simplistic Sumerian form into the more familiar "Mardukite" Chaldeo-Babylonian versions such as our archetypal *Creation Epic of Genesis*—the "*Enuma Elis*" and other ancient scriptures.

Seekers trying to blend multiple systems will be immediately confused—because modern practitioners interpret Lovecraft's "*Great Old Ones*" as planetary forces that the Mesopotamian work (represented by Simon, or our Mardukite "*Necronomicon: The Anunnaki Bible*") attribute to the "Elder Gods"—meaning the "younger pantheon" of *Anunnaki.* Is it possible that these are allusions to systems predating the Elder Gods? Probably not. These systems did not yet require sealing until the rise of the "Elder Gods."

Differing widely from historical viewpoints concerning Mesopotamian Anunnaki, the Lovecraftian interpretation regards two races of alien intelligence—"Ancient Ones" and the "Elder Gods." After what can only be described as a "primordial battle in heaven"—very similar to what we find in Babylonian literature and later Semitic scriptures derived from the same—the *Elder Gods* "seal" the *Ancient Ones* and entrap their powers into "gate-systems" that divides the material cosmos and "in the spaces between spaces."

In the end, the *Elder Gods* are allowed to rule the local universe. For moral and political justification, opposing forces are always demonized as monsters and "savage beasts" that must be destroyed to further the advancement or survival of a more "civilized" race.

In essence, the *"Great Old Ones"* of Lovecraft's visions, in their horrifying states, only loosely relate to the historic Anunnaki—the real "gods" of ancient humans. The "Elder Gods" are exactly that—these Anunnaki, known as gods, and particularly among them, the "younger pantheon" of Egypto-Babylonian systems, became the primary global influence thereafter in many cultural "mythologies."

This lore raises critical questions for those following traditions based on any aspect of the *Necronomicon* cycle, Lovecraftian or otherwise: Who or what do you serve? And is it a representation of the Highest? If we consider the *"Enuma Elis,"* the Anunnaki sealed away ancient primordial (possibly malignant) forces in order to create (or maintain) a material existence of *"Order."* If this necessary order also lends itself toward your own existential benefit: why would someone seek to dissolve this? Why consciously create uninhabitable conditions? The answer must reside within apocalyptic programs of "mortality" that are so deeply ingrained in human consciousness and its fragmented state when operated outside of *Self-Honesty*.

All systematic existence is *finite* from a physical or "mortal" point of view. Energy is constantly vibrating and forces are constantly in motion. According to Cosmic Law, *All* manifestation is fixed to a tidal ebb and flow cycle of action. We interact with only finite interpretations of these infinite forms and patterns. The trappings of the material system only demonstrate how limited things *can* be—not things as they *are*.

Whether or not the knowledge and experience of an individual is *Self-Honest*—free from the conditioning of the system—reality will continue to be justified (analytically or semantically) from the "memory pool" that you actually do have access to. "Conditioning" comes in an infinity of forms.

There are few answers for many Seekers discovering or realizing the *"Great Deception"* of material existence. Do we simply rebel against the physical as the Gnostics prescribe? Is this even a realistic approach? For those who fail to learn how to "live in the *kNow*," the focus on the mountaintop causes them to trip over what is right under their feet. There are movements, actions and beliefs that further your spiritual evolution toward the "goal"—and there are those which will not.

As an *Elder God* race—in either Lovecraft stories or Mesopotamian interpretations—these beings were able to fashion or manipulate a reality suitable for human habitation. In physical bodies, they interfaced with humans historically. But their own true natures are far from the familiar condensed energy vibrations of the "material."

Seemingly ageless and timeless entities from other worlds appear in some of the oldest known archetypal and genetic memories of humanity. These figures do not seem to have "created," so much as "systematized," the physical existence (and/or its conditions) of man—the arts of civilization—and the knowledge that propelled the race into what it has become. But it is now within the human psyche—its individualized nature—the means to interact with their environment, that has really caused the destruction and havoc that we see today.

The seed was planted from outside the system, but most humans have failed to see that they carry and unfold it themselves. There are many types of beings waiting to see *what* humans will "*unfold*."

In innumerable sources, the Elder Gods are represented with a pentagram—an earthly symbol of authority over material domains of five elements—but some believe it reveals the stellar origins of gods and humans. In esoteric occultism, the pentagram is used to represent man, and by nature, material existence.

Another frequently appearing symbol—the six-rayed star or "hexagram"—indicates communications between what is "seen" and "unseen"—or "physical" and "spiritual"—aspects of reality. This is evident in many of the popular Semitic-Kabbalistic "grimoires"—such as the *"Keys of Solomon"* cycle, &tc. A seven-pointed star is used to distinguish distant origins of the Anunnaki, beings that artistically depicted themselves with an eight-rayed star—the origin of the "asterisk," named for the Akkadian word for gods: "*istari.*"

If a system collapse were to take place—as sealed by the *Elder Gods* in these literary cycles—than the calamity that would follow would be nothing short than "un-creation." Whether because of their own bruised egos or some other even deeper source of spiritual malcontent, some have sought this "*Uncreation*" since the very beginning of ceremonial magic practices—a rebellious self-destruct system within the heart of an already rebellious counter-culture approach.

Rather than seek harmonious relationships with the guardian protectors of humanity—because of the type of person often attracted to these aspects—what is presented as "dark" and "recessed" seems to carry the widest appeal.

Whenever one wishes to knowingly embark upon a "dark" path —they have kind of set themselves up already. Any division of polarity in consciousness where one is clinging to a "negative" extreme, the same system is being followed—just backwards—an ebbing pendulum swing between extremes. The "good" only remains so if there is a "bad" to clash it against—otherwise, people get bored and easily begin to stop accepting the program. So long as forces are in motion, the program remains.

Since the time of ancient Sumer, nearly all traditions are based on perceptions of these forces as ever at odds with one another —but they are of a singular nature, primarily split or divided in human consciousness. It is only outwardly reflected as a "dual-party" system, but it is not.

The true battle over your "soul"—the unfoldement and evolution of the *Self*—is mainly: you against yourself. Can you rise from what you thought you were, into what you are supposed to be? The "humanistic" reply from the modern *Mardukite* movement, as expressed in "*Necronomicon: The Anunnaki Bible*":—

"Most practitioners who are drawn to these mysteries are not sympathetic to the destruction and malignant energies manifested on the planet by the human population—correctly dubbed by T.H. White as '*homo ferox*' in his *Book of Merlyn*. It seems to some that the only solution toward protecting the integrity of the "Big Picture"—even beyond another "seven generations"—requires reincorporation of the original source powers that brought this all into being at its start. Whether or not this energy can peacefully coincide with the current human systems in place—is the last of our concerns."

◊ ◊ ◊   ◊ ◊ ◊   ◊ ◊ ◊

The apocalyptic *"R'lyeh Text"* was not mentioned specifically in H.P. Lovecraft's writings. However, he suggests that the great priest of the Old Ones—*Cthulhu*—lies "dreaming" in the underground city of "R'lyeh," a sunken lost city in the ocean, that will rise again when "the stars are right." This other "book" separate from the *Necronomicon* was suggested by later writers and contributors to the "*Cthulhu Mythos*"—in this case, *August Derleth*.

Other similar tomes allegedly from the *Necronomicon* cycle have been introduced in related stories and tales for the past 100 years. Even if we did accept "research" from Lovecraftians, our other Mesopotamian Anunnaki records still predates all of this. The *"R'lyeh Text,"* by admission of those who believe in it, originates circa 300 B.C.—approximately the same time that one of the last true priests of Babylon—Berosus (Berossus)—chronicled the details of "*Oannes*"—*Dagon* or *Enki*. The "fictional" *Necronomicon* of the "Mad Arab" is only from the 7th century A.D.—well after Chaldeo-Babylonian, Semitic, Christian, Zoroastrian and Persian influences would all have had their influence on *any* understanding of the system.

Concerning Donald Tyson's "Lovecraftian" contributions—*"Necronomicon"* and *"Grimoire of the Necronomicon"*—seven forces are again singled out, such as we should expect, especially from an author skilled in ceremonial magic and Enochian practices. They are, of course, aligned to the system as planetary forces. There are, however, not very many esoteric practitioners seriously adhering to Tyson's method of "Lovecraftian Ritual Magic" today.

Throughout esoteric literature and occultism we repeatedly see the same correspondences apply to any seven-fold system—music, color, days of the week, &tc.—but this is all that grants Lovecraftian ritual magicians any "just cause" to celebrate a functional "*Cthulhu Mythos*" tradition.

But in the case of many of these "newer systems," it is the same universal tradition of planetary magic, *just* with Lovecraftian names—and just as applicable as if we were to ascribe Greek, Roman or some other language to this planetary system. Donald Tyson simply chose: Azathoth, Nyaralathotep, Yog-Sothoth, Yig, Shub-Niggurath, Cthulhu and Dagon for his descending pantheon. And here—where many Mesopotamian practitioners and esoteric scholars often associate Cthulhu with the historical Dagon, Tyson continues to separate this entity as yet another identity—as Lovecraft himself may have also mistakenly done.

The primary benefit to displaying a Lovecraftian interpretation across the "*Ladder of Lights*" is simply that we may more easily compare this version to the actual Babylonian luminous gate-system demonstrated in Mardukite materials based on historical sources.

For example, we can compare the following planetary associations made between Lovecraftian beings and those of the BAB.ILI system from Mesopotamia:—

Azathoth	Sun (Sol)	*Shammash* (or *Samas*)
Nyarlathotep	Mercury	*Nabu*
Yog-Sothoth	Jupiter	*Marduk*
Yig	Saturn	*Ninurta* (or *Ninib*)
Shub-Niggurath	Venus	*Ishtar* (or *Inanna*)
Cthulhu	Mars	*Nergal*
Dagon	Moon	*Nanna* (or *Sin*)

It should be clearly understood: Any properly designed planetary-based system of magic will work for that reason alone—regardless of what "names" are given to the specific currents.

For example, so long as the archetypal energy identified is identical one-to-one, the choice of language—*Zeus, Marduk, Yog-Sothoth, Dys Pater,* &tc.—is irrelevant if each is understood to mean: "*Jupiter.*" It is for this reason that people found any mutual success with planetary-aligned Enochian magic—in spite of many "inconsistencies" spread among various interpretations of *John Dee's* work.

The *Schlangekraft recension* includes a preface titled: "*Supplemental Material to 777*"—alluding to a kabbalistic reference work compiled by Aleister Crowley. It is a fascinating parallel derived from the "*Enuma Elis,*" but carries some astrological inconsistencies. However, prior to modern Mardukite work, this is the only direct attempt to connect Kabbalistic or occult associations to the Mesopotamian (Anunnaki) pantheon. It appears in Simon's work allegedly at the request of the O.T.O. (*Ordo Templi Orientis*) —or perhaps even Kenneth Grant, directly. Another version of the same lore was later circulated underground from on obscure group (real or imagined) calling themselves the "Order of the Silver Lotus." In any case, it will be of interest to those who study these matters.

[*A facsimile of this document appears on the next page.*]

SUPPLEMENTAL MATERIAL TO "777"

[Kabbalistic / Esoteric]	[Mesopotamian] {Lovecraftian}
0. -00-	Anu (Tiamat)
1. Primum (Crown)	Enlil (Absu) {Azathoth}
2. Zodiac (Wisdom)	Enki (Igigi) {Nyralathotep}
3. Saturn (Understanding)	Adar (Ninib) {Shub-Niggurath}
4. Sphere of Jupiter	Marduk
5. Sphere of Mars	Nergal
6. Sphere of the Sun	Utu (Shammash)
7. Sphere of Venus	Inanna (Ishtar)
8. Sphere of Mercury	Nebo (Nabu)
9. Moon (Foundation)	Nanna (Sin) {Cthulhu}
10. Elements (Malkuth)	Kia (Earth) {Ubbo-Sathala}
11. Air	Anna (Sky)
12. Mercury	Gudud (Nabu) {Nyralahotep}
13. Moon	Sin (Nanna)
14. Venus	Dlibat (Ishtar)
15. Aries	Agru (Xubur)
16. Taurus	Kingu (Moon)
17. Gemini	... (Viper)
18. Cancer	Shittu (Serpent)
19. Leo	... (Lakhamu)
20. Virgo	Shiru Whirlwind
21. Jupiter	Umunpaddu
22. Libra	Zibanit (Dog)
23. Water	Badur
24. Scorpio	(Scorpion-Man)
25. Sagittarius	(Hurricane)
26. Capricorn	(Fish-Man) {Yog-Sothoth}
27. Mars	Mastabarru
28. Aquarius	Gula (Horned Beast)
29. Pisces	(Weapon) {Dagon & Hydra}
30. Sun	Shammash (Samas)
31. Fire	Ag {Cthugha}
32. Saturn	Kaimanu {Tsathoggua}
33. Earth	Kia
34. Spirit	Zi

Quite simply, one of the only ways that Anunnaki *Necronomicon* lore and the Lovecrafitan *Necronomicon* lore can be mystically and esoterically compared is through observation of a common baseline. In the above given examples, the basic planetary orientation of the traditional Babylonian gate-system with the later Semitic Kabbalah—yet another gate-system derived from the same. But...

> *Tell the type of person painstakingly researching and devising such correspondences that "at the end of the day: all is one in equality" and they have a nervous breakdown on you.*

Whether under one set of semantics or another, the systems remain fixed—*static*—against the background of the cosmos—fixed by "Cosmic Law." It is this "background veil" that Seekers truly desire to pierce, but to do so is to acknowledge a whole messy labyrinth of systems and structures that one must sift through, recognize, and absolve. Kenneth Grant writes in *"Outer Gateways"*:—

> "The occultist has necessarily to revert to the 'primordial void' in order to encounter the source materialization."

Strictly "Lovecraftian" efforts, whether of fans or occultists alike, have actually failed to pierce the *Veil*—true "Crossing to the Abyss" is not among their most fundamental exploits. Where any threads do appear, they elusively shroud any useful coherency. A few scattered references appear in ambiguous work concerning "veils of negative existence" and also an Argentium Astrum (A.A.) initiation ritual designed by Aleister Crowley. Otherwise, mystical pursuits to self-honestly access the void are relayed more clearly in materials from the modern Mardukite movement. As explained in Mardukite *Liber 50*, it is the *"Primordial Abyss"* that represents the true background nature of existence—everything else is but colors on a screen, keeping the senses occupied in a fractured physical existence.

◊ ◊ ◊   ◊ ◊ ◊   ◊ ◊ ◊

Many learned scholars and esoteric leaders fall into the "system-trap," not because they consciously wish to propagate the deception of reality further, but because there are few other ways in which to communicate the information. To be any more "gnostic" in the relay runs risks of looking even "crazier" in an already "fluffy" metaphysical field of study, practice and writing —so very few of those who have become popular personas in the "New Age" are quick to "pull the rug out" from under their readers. Few are willing to sacrifice their income and livelihood for Truth.

If newly presented systems cannot continue to be packaged with mystical correspondences of various signs and symbols into new paradigms, then the whole mega-system would collapse. The masses are not ready for such a thing.

H. P. Lovecraft never saw his mythos as a fixed pantheon—it was left to others to do this, those that sought something practical and workable within the "ceremonial paradigm." Only some, it seems, have been a little more admitting about this than others. For example, in his "*Grimoire of the Necronomicon*," Donald Tyson writes:—

"Those familiar with Lovecraft's fiction may raise objection that he made no link between the Old Ones and the seven planetary spheres of traditional astrology. True enough. However, it has been a common practice in the Western esoteric tradition to use the symbol sets of astrology to categorize various groups of esoteric beings or occult qualities. This is not a modern conceit, but goes back many centuries. It was done because it was useful, for purely practical reasons, to make this kind of symbolic association. When the lords of the Old Ones are placed on the spheres of the planets, all the occult correspondences for the planetary spheres become available to use in summoning them and directing them in ritual work."

It is the hope of the current editor to resolve the mystery by citing the above reiteration. Because—there we have it: no matter what you do within the system, you are still within the rainbow of lights, playing at the game of alien intelligences. That this began in the ancient Babylonian system of planetary forces and designations has already become clear—but that we continue to interpret all of our mysteries solely from this guise is not so readily observed as people debate their preferred planet-names.

As with any classification or labeling venture, the systematized magicians cease to perceive raw ancient and primordial energy currents as they truly exist, and instead, are forced to see them through the veil of some other esoteric pattern. Nonetheless, contemporary magicians and practitioners have continued to dazzle themselves and each other with the seemingly infinite correspondences and relationships made between the same key elements under various names.

Perhaps the most liberating interpretation of the Mardukite work regarding the "Ladder of Lights" is to "work the system out." Rather than passively pathworking through the glamours and trying to maintain was is perceived, the "Gatework" derived from the Babylonian tradition is used by the modern practitioner to access "outside the system."

By leaving the "safety net" of the Realm of Light, you are no longer contained by its illusions. By not fully "Crossing to the Abyss," you have not been able to access any self-honest experience beyond the veils. Veils of existence are confronted and transcended in their entirety. Warnings connected notoriously to these mysteries speak against only accessing "some" of the veils. There are no half-measures to completion. Doing so leaves the practitioner lost between two world and unable to be withheld by either.

UNIVERSAL AGENTS OF SYSTEMOLOGY

A infinite spectrum of colors and lights—mysteries of reality and the nature of the universe—continue to captivate our minds. The need or craving to "know" is there—always there—programmed deeply within human consciousness, but the avenues are endless and often without "true" enlightenment.

The *"need to Know"* is so great that we can even manifest *things* to "Know" about. *Whatever the Thinker, thinks; the Prover, proves.* At the height of the initiatory pyramid, there is a genuine understanding of the material systems and veils of existence—but, what of it? Why is this esoteric pursuit of the "occult" so forbidding and sacred? And what spiritual evolution does it offer, beyond acquisition of mundane gratification?

The gods and spirits that are also a part of the system—what trappings await the Seeker that blindly supplicates before them? The "Solomonic" and "goetic" hierarchies—the demons and angels of the *"Book of Abramelin"*—to what do we owe these figures by prayer and sacrifice? Have they so easily deafened, as well as blinded, so that you cannot even hear their laughter?

It is possible that the Anunnaki may not be much different, but at the very least, a Seeker recognizes the raw energies as they are—to be equally "realist" and "metaphysicist," and call a spade: "a spade." And our modern "Mardukite" efforts are not in creating or transposing a new mythology—but instead, returning to the most ancient and original ones.

It should be understood through and through that in spite of the cosmological stories attached to them, the ancient *"gods"* are not the "Source"—not the "Creatrix" of a purely spiritual system. They are, instead, grand manipulators of the system, and for this feat alone they are called "gods." Some have even called them "dream-walkers" or "time-travelers" of the reality we inhabit. They have abilities to move through an additional "astral" dimension. We often imagine them inhabiting this additional dimension, moving through "time-space" as fluidly as our own freedom of movement in this energetically condensed material reality.

"Mardukite" priests of ancient Babylon were, by nature, *Priests of Enki*, following a derivative of ancient *systems* born in *Eridu*—the prehistoric capital city of *Enki*, located near the Persian Gulf sea. Beyond the *collected data* to support a belief system, the first pragmatic mystical and religious use of writing was the recording of *incantations*. Examination of these tablets reveals *appeals* to the *gods* for assistance in material matters. [Examples may be found in *Liber 50* and *Liber 51/52* and *The Complete Book of Marduk by Nabu*, all of which are collected in the hardcover Master Edition anthology: "*Necronomicon: The Complete Anunnaki Legacy.*"]

At the inception of "prehistoric" *Anunnaki* traditions, the people were instructed to petition their needs to the temple-priests—who in turn make appropriate offers and ritualized incantations necessary to enact "magic" of the *deity* involved. A distinction existed between the public "exoteric" religion observed by the general population and the "esoteric" one covertly practiced by the priests themselves.

New "historic" traditions resulted from unique dynamics made possible with the introduction of *cuneiform* writing into human consciousness—a time when things ceased to be seen solely from experience based learning and were instead rooted in language and data classification or "systematization." These dynamics of a "Mardukite" state or empire were not necessarily ruled by *Marduk* directly, but all of *Babylonia* existed under his care—and watchful eye—by way of the temple-priests and Kings serving in his name.

The modern "Mardukite" movement—and even the more recent developments of "Mardukite Zuism"—emphasizes research into historic systematization but does not propagate a religious systems revival in the manner typical of what most people think of, or expect, concerning "religion" and "dogma." Evolution of planetary systems—particularly human systems—is simply an *unfoldment* of program-designs playing out. It is not necessarily what is truly intended by "Higher Orders," but simply the way things developed by necessity to bring us here to these considerations of the Physical Universe and nature of its material existence that we experience from the perspective—or point-of-view—of the Human Condition.

"Authorities" shaped a prison to contain the human psyche—a vehicle for human sensory experience—further feeding the systematic program by continuously confirming its own very existence. In this way, the Seeker should come to see *Cosmic Law* just like the "Forces of Nature" or "Natural Law" more easily observed locally on the planet. This is actually one reason why mystics so heavily emphasize "getting back to Nature"—because all of the lessons we need to know about the universe are perfectly reflected there for the *Self* to experience.

Nature is a "system" of life—on earth, called an "eco-system." The more *"Elven-Faerie"* or *"Druidic"* paths of esoteric mystery put expressly put forth an idea that the entire earth planet operates as a single living organism—some call *"Gaea"* or *"Gaia."* Of course, from our perspective it has "relatively" smaller systems and larger ones, but all are integrated into one single program running its course.

There is some reason, then, to believe that the earth planet itself is an integral part of a "larger" working universal system. All cosmic systems in *Nature* exist for survival—a pendulous ebb and flow motion of necessity. It is not concerned with what is considered "pleasurable" and "cruel" to an individual—the program simply exists so that it may exist, and once installed, it is simultaneously connected to all of the other programs in existence.

All of this composes a single fractal "reality," where systems are "stacked" and perceived separately. Thus, subjectively there is a limited amount of information attainable of the *whole* from any *one* vantage point—and yet at the same time, a fractal signature or blueprint pattern of the whole is contained everywhere at once.

Many "mystics" observe a fundamental pattern inherent in *Nature*. Some have call it "gnomonic" or plot its ratios against various "phi" sequences—like the one famously "discovered" by the mathematician, Fibonacci. Others simply call it a "golden spiral" or compare it to the flow of electrons around an atom... or planets in a system... or even the star patterns in galaxies— nothing is truly random.

Wizards and mystics are not above "causal determinism"—and, in fact, they welcome its acknowledgment. This very observation of causal energy patterns is how we make things happen and even "predict" future events based on the randomity encountered in the Physical Universe.

Embracing knowledge of "Cosmic Law," as pertaining to mental and spiritual existence, gives one the ability to consciously (intentionally) create change—for how else would you even know to do so? What else gives you reason to believe that acting "now" in a specific way affects future events? Have you not already experienced the potential future before it takes place? Such awareness divides "bookshelf sorcerers" and "armchair wizards" from the true and intentional Self-determined "*reality engineers.*"

In one sense, there was a way that the common individual would have experienced the outward "exoteric" expression of *Anunnaki* tradition in Babylon and throughout Mesopotamia; and then, there was an entirely different "esoteric" reality experienced by those few in society who were directly charged by the "gods" to execute or *feed* this experience to the general population.

The modern Mardukite revival works from both angles—with "*The Anunnaki Bible*" containing a significant portion of the "public" or "classical" perception of Babylonian tradition in Mesopotamia. Supplemental work—such as Mardukite *Liber-50* and *Liber-51/52*—focuses on what lingers in the shadows of ancient Babylon—what is not necessarily a part of the "common knowledge" or integrated into the system in a way that people would readily see or perceive. We have even established an "advanced systemology" for those seeking to go further and discover the magic *behind* magic.

Anyone can "operate" in reality—the system was designed to "go"—but not everyone shares the same aptitude of what the system design really is, or the history (and identity) of the designers, or perhaps, more importantly, the knowledge to "tweak" (or "adjust") it. All of this has been carefully guarded and sealed behind what even the modern "New Age" interpretation of esoteric lore has failed to grasp.

The systems—*all systems*—are self-serving: based upon and existing to further propagation and survival of "the system." For the most part, systems in the universe are essentially "fixed" by *Cosmic Law*. But as modern generations know, the material system itself is more like a "shell" or simply the computer "hardware" that is waiting for a "program" to run. It is actually the "programs"—installed into natural systems governed by *Cosmic Law* that were manipulated by ancient Anunnaki gods during interactions with the material world at the inception of (modern) human civilization.

There are actually many order of being and life consciousness fragments in existence throughout the cosmos, but it was a specific group (called generically "Anunnaki" in Mesopotamian language) that is responsible for installation of the current programs in place all over the planet.

Once Babylonian politics entered the fray, and perhaps even before this, "lots" were drawn deciding the hierarchy of the local universe. But, the "younger generation" of "Elder Gods," and their ancestors or "Ancient Ones," all failed on this. Responsibilities for operating these installed programs, which were handed off to specific alleged lineages and cultures for care-taking, were also all mishandled—*miserably*.

This present age—approximately the last 2,000 years—actually started on a simple and beautiful premise brought to Earth by another wise messenger from the sky gods. But men misunderstood gravely—and failing to accept programming of this new freedom, nailed it to a cross. Humans decided to continue *fucking the program up* to the extent of even invoking the name of this peaceful warrior as a guise for corrupting it. Strange words for an occult text? *...Truth is Truth.*

Skeptics and occultists alike wonder why the *Anunnaki gods* do not materialize in the world as they once did—but look what this world would do to them? Do you think *Enlil, Enki* or *Marduk* wants to be nailed to a tree for your ignorance? *Hardly.* As we have not had much luck in "debugging" the program—the current push by the sons and daughters of the Anunnaki and their followers is toward a complete "system reboot" on planet Earth. In the meantime, we continue to advance Truth Seekers on an experiential path of *true knowledge* contributing to the unfoldment of personal spiritual evolution—and abilities that may develop as a result.

The program is flawed—there is no argument there. However, without the matrix-system in place, there is no fractured existence from the All. We would all cease to be "I" and would be a part of the universal consciousness as one—as we truly are, water-molecules in an infinite *Sea of Abyss.* One way or another, it would seem we are facing a powerful transitional "death" threshold—and Anunnaki "powers" are guarding all the doors and holding all the keys in this matter. They are the "Universal Agents" of the *Great Magical Arcanum* in this universe—"agents" existing to protect the system, just as this energetic "cosmic grid" also protects their own existence, or more accurately, the "ambiguity" of it.

Early on in this present work we focused on "initiatory lessons" and summations of what has come before; and with these being complete, the additional points of ambiguity faced here at the end only proves that the Seeker *is* ready for the next "level" or "degree" of clarity—for we already examined enough under this lens-magnification of our microscope...or *macroscope.*

If the theatre lights are brought up too early,
the audience might see the strings.

Systems are universal—they are everywhere and plentiful. We cannot so much fault their existence as the programs that they run. With rising human populations and their division into distinct geographical cultures and time, the "Great System" became increasingly the *Great Deception*—as its operation could be bent to meet the needs of the masses, or those that governed them. But, the deception is not really a matter of "morality," though many have called it "*Darkness.*" It is a direct result of the "chaos factor" inherent in *all* systems.

With time and without proper care, all systems break down from their programs... the entropy of forms returning to the *Infinity of Nothingness* in as eternal as the formation of new systems. But, somehow, they all seem to... "eat" themselves—Ouroborus—*the serpent dragon of the universe devours its own tail. And at the center of all existences—a black hole to the Beyond.*

PIERCING THE DARKNESS

So often we may have heard the phrase: "The devil made me do it!"—and to this, a response is generated, subject to the beliefs of the masses—or the "Realm"—in that time-space. At one juncture in history, such accusations of witchery on neighbors could result in the instant death of the innocent. Today, civil law generally operates by more scientific, and less religious or superstitious, occupations of the Realm—and thus, lore of psychology, not the *Malleus Maleficarum*, has become the governing gospel for "witchcraft."

It is curious that the ideal of modern "witchcraft" is increasingly pop-cultural in the "New Age," when such has held widely negative overtones throughout history. Even in our lore from the most ancient mysticism in Mesopotamia and Sumer, the official magical tradition of "temple-priests," "priestesses" and "magicians" is treated separate from unsanctioned operations used by "witches" and "sorcerers" *outside* civic regulation. This is especially evident when examining the complete *Maqlu* tablet series—given as *Mardukite Tablet M* within *"Necronomicon: The Anunnaki Bible"* (and available as a stand-alone volume as *"The Maqlu Ritual Book"* edited by Joshua Free).

Nearly two decades ago, while the current author pursued origins of the *Druidic* and *Pheryllt* traditions of the Celts—described within *Liber-D "Elvenomicon"* and companion volumes within that cycle of materials, including *"Draconomicon"* and *"Druid's Handbook"* by Joshua Free—an observed distinction came into view between the "holy temple" and "urban religious" magic systems versus "country-oriented" and "rural folk" traditions. These two classes clearly approach the esoteric path differently.

From the first stream there is a sense of "god-given" power used to oversee worldly matters, bestowed on civic priests, priestesses—those serving the Divine by maintaining observation of "*Cosmic Law.*" On the other hand, there are indigenous rural folk traditions embedded in the ancestral genetic history of all cultures, based on common observation of both *priestcraft* and "*Natural Law.*" This class distinction of esoteric mysteries is still carried among the "New Age" traditions today.

After the original ancient "gods" were gone from earth, the approach to esoteric mysteries shifted away from the Divine. The people forgot about the gods themselves, feeling abandoned and left to a intermittently crashing reality system—and it seemed that the gods forgot about the people, at least in the external manner they had expressed "watching over" them in the past. Where the systems and genetics remained, reliance on "divine intervention" subsided.

Human populations increased and by necessity the philosophies and politics changed to accommodate diverse culture formation. To support the evolution of rapidly growing civilizations, social-consciousness programs had to be "upgraded" as so to keep the system from collapsing. More complicated and intricately woven system-programs were required—and with complexity came a rise in entropic chaos factors and the spread of "*Darkness.*"

Those who work with these mysteries grow beyond the mere "mortal" understanding of good and evil—as without such self-honesty, the exploration of the "*Great Mysteries*" and the "*Great Deception*" become at once impossible.

"Darkness" is a name given to the balancing equation of the system that is not contained by the "Light," which from a physical perspective, is interpreted as the "Shadows." This is something beyond moral associations of "good" or "bad"—the Darkness is merely the force (or a name given to the force) that binds all programs now driving what the Gnostics describe as a "*Great Deception*"—that which keeps systems of physical material existence in place. It is both: the "spaces between spaces" and the "ghost in the machine" at once.

Darkness and *Deception*—much like *witchcraft* and *sorcery*—are often considered "negative" terms. Curiously, our understanding of each of these aspects are based on "*fear*" and the "*unknown*"—"*inexperience*" and "*ignorance*." Certainly, it is too cliché to simply say, as many have, that "people are afraid of what they do not understand." But, considering how experiential existence projects from "Self," it is necessarily the case that people feed experiences with personal reactive-responses, thereby creating a "resonance loop" with specific concepts. This impression or resonance is not just felt within the "reality" of the person experiencing it directly—it can be shared and it can spread.

The larger the system and the more programs being run, the greater the chance for obscurity—the *chaos factor*. As more and more people became aware of this (and began feeding it), this too became "sentient" as its own program—*and now people can even interact with it directly!*

Few things in the universe are as they seem. Their appearance is often based on what the observer sees—their own perceptions. These perceptions may not change what things *actually* are, but people do actually interact with their world based on perceptions from previous experiences and this affects the way things seem. By necessity, this is unavoidable in semantic classifications of reality and also necessary to preserve "deceptions" of the programs.

So long as people are distracted by their own internal processes of experience, the aspects that drive and perturb these experiences remain behind the curtain—leaving the observer to merely interact with the "voice" and "image" projected on the screen.

True manifestations of "Darkness" are not usually what we might expect—not even a proper descriptive term for the nature of the beings or creatures themselves. They are understood only to the extent that experiences are interpreted and interacted with. If they *are* the horrors and macabre "you might expect," it is very possible that they are not being encountered Self-Honestly.

When approached with false knowledge, fear and/or without confidence, any and all aspects of the cosmos can quickly become a "*devil*" to you—at least from the perspective of Ego. Occult author, Leilah Wendell, writes in "*The Books of Azrael*":—

> "All spiritual energy is originally formless. However, it harnesses the necessary knowledge, understanding and ability power to transmute itself into visible form. As with psychokinesis, where simple underdeveloped human psychic energy emissions can influence matter and movement, imagine what mastery an ancient spiritual and divine being can have over the energy that is its very life-force!"

While applicable as a fundamental tenet, Leilah Wendell's commentary on manifestation is specifically related to lore of her encounters with "*Azrael*"—the "Angel of Death" in the Semitic interpretation of the ancient mysteries. She interprets this energy current as a necessary part of existence—the force that separates the "spirit-form" from the "body" when a creature-being approaches the "*Death-Gate*" of their current material lives. She goes on to explain that while originally a "formless" body of energy, these spiritual intelligences, much like ourselves, have the ability to condense their energy into recognizable forms. These forms can take on a sort of *timeless* "archetypal familiarity"—thus while abstract, "Death" is universally portrayed as a recognizable form—the Grim Reaper or "Time"—throughout history. Wendell continues, explaining:—

> "If the familiar image were greatly altered, the being would be *deceiving* the viewer; and the Universal Soul does *not* deal in *deceptions*. That is the realm of an opposing force altogether."

All manifestations of "Darkness" are something of an ambiguity when we look upon and experience them outside of Self-Honesty. Again, it is not so much a description of these forces in themselves, but instead how they are perceived in the reality of lights and encoding that can reveal no "negative spaces between." But, too, all programming can be corrupted.

Consider the example given elsewhere in these discourses concerning the appearance of Jesus and his liberating teachings two-thousand years ago. When esoterically examining the actual teachings of Jesus, there is little debate concerning their spiritual validity. But it is not an understanding of these esoteric teachings themselves that are openly expressed by the traditional "Christian" program (paradigm)—which cannot allow individuals to be liberated independent of the "Church."

The systems governing the present state of the Human Condition—all worldly material systems really—spawns "slavery," and so anything that might be liberating (e.g. the true teachings of Jesus) must therefore be corrupted in order for the program to maintain existence in the Realm. *Hiding Truth in plain sight.* The torch of esoteric *Truth* may continue to be carried by the select few—but never by everyone. We cannot necessarily tip the scales of mass-consciousness as an ends in itself—and that is not really our goal. Therefore, in this instance, we can say that the system was revised to allow for "Christianity," meanwhile opposing forces continue to use whatever means necessary for survival—*even the teachings of Christ.*

◊ ◊ ◊   ◊ ◊ ◊   ◊ ◊ ◊

The current generation has little difficulty understanding that the "self" is an operator (or "user") of a "program" in a "system." It begins to sound like something out of *The Matrix* or *Thirteenth Floor* or even *Tron*. Folks have been attempting to systematically relate the human condition to "computers" for some time. Prior to this semantic availability, behaviorist psychology understood similar via their paradigm of "conditioning"—but there is a higher state of awareness beyond physical reactions alone. Proof is evident that physical reality is very much the product of "conditioning"—the *"whys"* and *"hows"* remain elementary, confined to an understanding using "paradigms." All energetic implications beyond the spectrum of "normal" human perceptions—maintained as a "materialist program"—are not understood in existing contemporary methodologies that rely solely on materialist programs.

Understanding the *Self* is not different from relatively under-standing the "cosmic whole"—as many mystics have gone forth to explain that they are one and the same. The key is looking at the integrated web-matrix structure of all existence—all of which operates under the same "Cosmic Laws."

We observe multiple "systems" within a "System" and all of these are programmed. What we call "fragmentation" is subject-ively a way of looking at the divisible aspects of creation as "parts" when classifying and communicating "reality" within any program or "paradigm." There is a pure energetic Source that exists outside of all definitions within the system and so while our true nature may not be separated, the experience of it within this condensed material existence appears to be—hence *fragmentation*.

Elsewhere in *NexGen Systemology* literature, we liken *Self-Honesty* to "crystal clarity." The experience of *Self* as a "programmed crystalline fragment" is also very similar to the idea of pro-grams encoded onto a crystal computer chip. It is so similar, in fact, that we have often found it best to define it this way for modern purposes.

At one level of perception, a computer as a whole is a system of material hardware—at another it is a system to run programs. During the casual "user experience" of computers, one does not generally encounter the entirety of background programming on the surface—the actual code embedded "behind" the experi-ence displays only a predetermined "user interface." And it is also *interactive*—within a fixed set of parameters in which to ex-perience itself, but *fluid* and *dynamic* all the same.

The user is limited to system parameters of the program and more often then not, the full capabilities or potential extent of "unfixed" parameters is not experienced by a user. And much like a personal identity, the system becomes increasingly "re-fined" as *individuality*—by everything from the actual "operating system" used, to the "programs" run, and of course the available space, speed and methodology by which any of this is accessed. Enter further the personal experience of the user and their personality and you can easily see that even the same piece of "hardware" or system is going to be used, accessed and perceived differently by each user, themselves. *This is why the Rabbit Hole of perceived reality appears to run so deep...*

"Light" is essentially the *language* that cosmic existence is encoded in. This not only includes personal identities, but all "manifested" existence within the "visible" spectrum of experience. We mean not only "visual appearances" but the entire base for an "*observer*" to perceive what they experience as their own existence, separate from "other" or "outer" existences.

In short, the "inner world" and "outer world" are thought of as separate identities, even among many "New Age" schools, and this furthers the perception (or "deception") of such as "fragments." Rather than holding the belief that some "outside reality" has an affect on an "internal reality" and that an "inner realm" can affect an "outer realm," the mystic realizes that they are one and the same "reality"... *since any separation would contradicts how and why all things are indeed connected in agreement as this universal reality—All as One.*

Although there is only one interconnected existence, the program as given to individual "beings" forces them to interpret reality based on semantic "levels" *within* and *without* a visible (communicable) spectrum to experience. Sensory stimulus is used to increase all personal programming through experience. Personal programming contributes to the total shared *Akashic Pool* or "global consciousness"—just like the world-wide-web. Everything we come to experience is also imprinted within our coding of existence. In many ways these energetic signatures and imprints begin to define us and our existential experience of our environment—albeit artificially.

Our entire mental "bank" is a repository for potential conscious thought. Few are able to recognize this effect during their lifetime. Higher "routes" of Mardukite Systemology emphasize a direct resolution of response-reactive encoding even further. But, quite simply, when we come right down to the base knowledge of such, we are again returned to this concept of *Light*.

Cosmic Law is universal. The programming of our own forms is the same as the programming of forms we encounter—perceived to be separate—and all of this is programmed in *Light*. In fact, our main New Age conceptualization of this programming in the "New Age" revives *Eastern* ideals following this logic—auras and chakras—an entire personal energetic system composed of what? ...*Light!* All experience in existence and conscious memory of it in pictures and sounds are primarily waves or frequencies of what? ...*Light!*

And what you consciously retain as "memory" is only an awareness experienced within a fixed set of parameters, a predefined scope limit, we tend to call the "Human Condition." But this does not mean that relatively "unseen" directives are not also in action, simply in bands of *Light* that are not so visible and consciously retained—but they are not any less "real." Is it not possible that our finite world of lights is the "*shadow*" of something even more "Absolute"...?

◊ ◊ ◊   ◊ ◊ ◊   ◊ ◊ ◊

All individualized fragments or "identities" are programmed with a base "operating system" so as to interpret a world around them. By definition, the way reality is experienced compliments and builds upon this preset programming.

Additional programming or "updates" will either "enhance" or "override" what already exists—but most often these strongly encoded imprints become a very active part of the program—directly influencing the way life is experienced by a spiritual entity. It also influences what is not expressed—the totality of existence—regardless of our awareness of what is taking place "behind the scenes," yet just as real.

We have mentioned "light encoding" manifesting as personal auric and chakra systems that exist, but they seem outside the small part of the "spectrum" condensed enough to be considered "physical" in the typical sense of the word. At the same time, they share a relationship with all aspects of this Realm—because *All is One*. They do not exist at some separate "level" in exclusion. It is the same "level" and "existence"—vibrations that simultaneously exist at all "levels"—*as One*—but each frequency-type of the wave is senses and experienced differently by different organs of the body—whether "sensory" in a strictly "material" sense or otherwise.

What we experience as reality is a combination of expressions—visible forms of light and audible forms of sound are wave vibrations which interpreted within strict guidelines by specific personal faculties—eyes for light and ears for sound, &tc. But, of course, we already know that these ranges vary between different people and also different species. This allows for the same reality to be experienced differently by individually fragmented entities—*hence, the crystalline perception!*

"New Age" definitions of the "physical" versus the "metaphysical" and the "material" versus the "spiritual" are based in an idea that there are both *sensibly* visible (seen) and invisible (unseen) forces at work in the universe. These particularly affect experiences by energetic beings—like *humans*. However, too often, Seekers become lost in a labyrinth of "levels" and "layers" that are so vastly distinguished in exclusion to one another throughout contemporary literature.

The more widespread the *Great Mysteries* reached on the planet and in the cosmos, the more "complex" the *Great Deception* had to become in order to contain it. It is sometimes difficult to morally decide who the "good guys" are versus the "bad guys." It is all an integral of the same system—one type merely breeds more of the same. Without operating temperance in the exponential rise of programs, a greater "chaos factor" forms within them, supporting an increased population of those who continue to propagate what most would consider "negative" energy.

But, this seems somewhat different than a worldview where cosmic forces of *Light* and *Dark* are endlessly pitted against one another, locked in some moral warfare over your soul. In another instance, these forces exist for no other reason than to provide the illusion of movement—the ebb and flow of the

112

pendulum swing of universal energy. One without the other does not create this "motion of activity" and as such will not hold programming. We must not demonize the hidden recesses or celebrate myriads of color. *All is one in equality.*

When someone is cooking in a room other than where you are, you might smell the food and therefore have a sensory reaction with reality—or what you perceive of reality. The source of this, is however, somewhere other than where you have access to visually or with your "material" body—but the experience is still thought of as "real" or within your "reality." There is no question to you, because of your previous experience, that someone "real" exists in another room you "don't see" that is the cause of this. With more "experience" you might even have already distinguished both the person and the type of food being prepared —but these are all things within your field of knowing.

These are what people call "levels" of reality—duality between "seen" and "unseen" factors—but they are actually all one reality—one existence. While still within the light spectrum, there are parts of the program that are happening outside our field of view. These still affect us—and we affect them. Based on the above example, imagine if you did not have previous experience with the way that food smells drift, &tc. Even if this is a rudimentary example at best, you should be now realize its implications.

"There are more things in heaven and earth than are dreamed of in your philosophies..." All experiences carry with them aspects that are not within the "normal" human range of sensory experience. These are aspects that the "hardcore materialists" have considered "fictional fantasy" in their reality. Since they have no direct experience with it, it cannot be real to them. But this does not change the fact that energetic aspects will affect them anyway—and the Clear Light is bent and fragmented in a way they are programmed to receive.

Those not yet evolved enough to process esoteric knowledge do not seem to miss it. Whether or not they are privy to forces behind what happens to them in their lives becomes irrelevant.

So much the better if—allegedly: *the greatest trick the devil ever played was convincing the world he didn't exist. . .*

The *Great Deception* prevails. For those who don't know to look for it—are programmed to reject the "non-material"—the *Great Mystery* does not even exist at all. For those who go in pursuit of it, there are enough trappings along the way to distract them— and even many who reach the top only reach self-deluded points of "pseudo-enlightenment."

Some are seeking their way to get "outside"—others don't really know it exists, and they are barely aware of their own waters in which they swim. To the best that is determinable from our perspective of the crystal—it is the *Anunnaki*—that appear to be holding the keys and guarding the gates of this existence.

So now you have been show the *door*—and where you go from here is up to you. What you do with it and where you take it— these are the decisions only your own programming can de- termine.

What is good or bad?

Who are the saviors?

—Which way is up. . ?

If you've been paying attention,

then you will figure it out...

◊ ◊ ◊　　◊ ◊ ◊　　◊ ◊ ◊

This section excerpts the complete Mardukite Tablet Catalogue for *Liber-9*.
These materials have since been incorporated into
"Necronomicon: The Anunnaki Bible" and "The Complete Anunnaki Bible"
and *"Necronomicon: The Complete Anunnaki Legacy"* 2020 Master Edition.
They appear here as they did in the 2011 limited edition of *"Novem Portis."*

THE BOOK OF HEADACHES & DEMONOLOGIE
(Tablet-H)

The ancient world would appear, at first glance, to be composed of little else but fictitious "evil spirits" and the superstitious fools that fuel them with belief. To take the naïve historian's or mythographer's perspective might be convenient to some—but to a Seeker of the True Words, we cannot succumb to such surface interpretations. Complete records of the infamous Maklu (*Maqlu*) "Burning" Tablets make an appearance elsewhere in the *Necronomicon Anunnaki Bible* [and in "*The Maqlu Ritual Book*" edited by Joshua Free], but the Seeker may be less aware of other tablet series from similar origins, mainly: *Surpu* ("Consuming Demons"), *Utukku Limnuti* ("Book of Evil Spirits"), *Ti'i Tii* ("Book of Headaches"), *Asakki Marsuti* ("The Fevers & Sickness"), *Labarto* ("The Hag-Demon").

In the Babylonian system, a priesthood, called ASIPU or MAS-MASU, is dedicated to exorcisms and banishment of ill-fortune (thought to be from people's thoughts and deeds themselves, or those of another—e.g. wicked sorcerer). Uninitiated wicked sorcerers and witches are those practicing "illegal magic" (sorcery) outside the "realm" without permission for personal gain or against society. Only the temple-priesthood could practice magic. These true "wizards" and "witch-doctors" were actually given a highly esteemed class-status for their abilities in combating against the "evil" sorcery cast by the lower class "hostile" and "wicked" ones.

"Words of Power" associated with both the subtle conjuring of the "daemons" or the violent exorcisms of the "evil genius"— whether it be by the *Most Holy Roman Catholic Ritulae* or the most diabolic of grimoires (e.g. the "Grand Grimoire" and "Dragon" grimiores—which occupy the same mythological paradigm as Catholicism and Judaism) are always of the "highest"—or else to say: "Holy Names" (e.g. Tetragrammaton). This is because the vibrations of the Material World occupy under the governance of the Material Ruler or Lord of the Earth,[1] which may have appeared in the past as a "Source God" but of which is only a "cyclic god."

It is "Supernal Trinities" and "Unspeakable Names" that carry the avenging hunter and glorifying worshiper of "daemon" shadow along their way. And the wise appear to use the systematic hierarchy of the "highest" to achieve these ends. For in the ancient times we see priests of ERIDU and BABYLON calling to MARDUK to appeal to his farther ENKI. By the time of the Jewish mystics, such as we find in the "*Book of Abramelin*," this title has been generalized to "Adonai," meaning simply, "Lord," though fundamentalist monotheists can only perceive the notion as "God–Source." Catholic priests and Christian sciences adopt the name of "Jesus" as Adonai for the Piscean Age, something that many occultists actually find logical.

No different then we find among the cornucopia of anecdotal paranormal experiences today, the ancients had their run-ins with what con-temporary society once generalized as "ghosts"— meaning the ethereal spiritual presence of an ancestral ("dead") spirit, or rather an spirit that returns due to its "unrest" or difficulty in "crossing." These are called "*edimmu*" ("E.DI.IM.MI") in Babylonian (Assyrian) lexicons. Another is called the "*utukku*."

Later interpreted to be a "daemon" (without being distinguished for its beneficent nature), the "*lamassu*" is a "positive" guardian spirit that is called forth in many of the tablet rites. It is hard to separate, in all cases, the difference between this spirit and the "*sedu*" guardian, but the combined lore of these led to the later Assyrian belief in "guardian angels" that carried over into modern Judeo-Christian beliefs.

---

1   "Lord of the Earth" (of the Physical Universe) meaning "Lord of this World"— traditionally ENKI. Considered the "Demiurge" of the Gnostic tradition. Sometimes equated with Satan.

A knowledge of the elements of both the Material World and the spiritual one is essential for priestcraft. The function of "healer" often fell upon temple-priests. Tablets show evidence for a practice of spiritual medicine coupled with lore of natural cures, such as is revived in contemporary medicine. The "elements of life," appear physically and figuratively in ritual observances— specifically the "waters of life" and the "fires of life" which are considered purifying and cleansing, but also deceptively destructive. The "blood of life" and "breath of life" are also iconic ceremonial and spiritual symbols found in many religious mythologies.[2]

Concerning "bans" or "tabu" ("taboo") of ancient tradition— many such are placed on aspects of healthy and sanitary living. For example, the more obvious include contact with the body of a corpse... or of a woman who is menstruating... or the body of a young maiden girl... It is these social restrictions, taboos or "bans" that are placed on "civilized" man as a means of preserving order. Alleged "mind daemons" also appear to await us around every corner seeking to thwart the hearts and actions of men away from adhering to the Law. Whatever the nature of such might be, when someone does go "against the grain" bringing chaos into a given system, repercussions (even in the form of "thought-formed daemons") emerge.

The role of "sympathetic magic" in these affects cannot be overlooked. Given the vivid descriptions we have been given to draw off from ancient tablets, we see evidence for the stereotypical "voodoo-doll" as perhaps the most ancient recorded "folk charm"—used to represent a psychic target for either side as they essentially may be used to curse or remove curses or heal. Representative figures made of wax and other substances frequently appear. In fact the Book of Burnings & the Maklu (or *Maqlu*) can even be seen as a literal embodiment of the burning, melting, waxen images: Ceremonial burnings in metaphoric effigy are usually performed with waxen dolls "made in the image of your enemy." Elsewhere it explains that "a waxen doll may be cursed over a flame and then melted into a cauldron." The idea of connecting to the spirit or "soul" of a being via some waxen

---

2   This is also discussed in *"The Vampyre's Handbook"* by Joshua Free.

or natural-made image can be found in mystical practices of Babylonians, Egyptians and early Semitic tribes.

There are significant "sympathetic" powers attained via the knowledge and use of one's name—which is to say the "true-name"—of a spirit or entity (embodied or not). As *R.C. Thompson* writes (paraphrasing *Lejean*): "The modern Abyssinian believes in demons being constantly on the watch to steal a Christian's name if they can, and it is the custom to conceal the real name by which a person is baptized with." In the Egyptian Grimoire translated by *Budge*, a rite is described by which both aspects of these powers are combined in combating the daemon "APEP"[3] – a waxen figure is made in his image along with the name being written thereupon. The charm is burned as a means of "binding" the spirit, although the text reads: "destroy."

Semantic connections between "cleanliness" and "sanity" can be traced back to roots of the word, but to clarify further: ideas of uncleanliness, sin and demons are all synonymous among the ancients. Violation of health taboos also contributed to visible consequences also connecting cleanliness and sin. Origins of this lore may have begun as ceremonial inclinations. Morgenstern describes in *Doctrine of Sin in Babylonian Religion*—"the expressions: sin, uncleanliness, sickness, possession by evil spirits, are pure synonyms. They denote an evil state of the body, the result of the divine anger...sin must have been originally purely ritual. Either the man had neglected to offer his sacrifice, or else had not offered it properly." It is important to note that before sacrifices could be offered properly, a person would have first needed a "ritual cleansing" – furthering again a combined significance of purity.

MARDUK'S ANUNNAKI MANDALA OF PROTECTION

MARDUK has seen him. [meaning, the "sick one"]
MARDUK has gone to the house of his father, ENKI.
MARDUK asked of ENKI: "The headaches, whence

---

3   APEP—the Egyptian version of the primordial chaos "dragon" called TIAMAT in Mesopotamia and also TYPHON to others.

comes it?"
And ENKI responded: "You know it is from the
[Underworld], my son."
MARDUK asked of ENKI: "What this ailing man has done,
he knows not.
How may he be relieved from this [Underworld curse]?
And ENKI responded: "My son, what you do not know now,
I cannot give you.
My knowledge has already been added to your own.
Go now."
But before MARDUK departed, ENKI did divulge to him
the secrets...

◊ ◊ ◊   ◊ ◊ ◊   ◊ ◊ ◊

(Description: To be said in the magick circle by the priest who
has fashioned seven winged figures to place before him.)

Directions for the practitioner:
  To spread a dark garment on their "upraised arms."
  To bind the arms of the patient (or cursed one).
  To mark the "*usurtu*"[4] boundary with the sprinkling of lime."
  The "*usurtu*" must also be marked by the "*Flour of Nisaba.*"

Incantation of Ceremonial Affects:
  "At the head of these seven figures with the terrible wings
["fearful wings"], I have set a figure of NERGAL. I have conjured
NUZKU ["*nusku*" the Fire-God] at their head in the [cauldron]—
AGA MASS SSARATU. Twin figures ["guardians", "wards"] I have
set to over-whelm the ["evil spirit"] at the right and left side of
the ["sick", "possessed"] man. In the foundations of this place I
have set the ["ward"] of LUGAL-GIRRA ["Lord of the Fires of GIB-
IL", "Lord of the Fires of Heaven-God"] of which there is no
rival. Beneath the bed [where lays the "injured"]."

  "I have set the figure of NARUDU, Sister of the Elder Gods
[who is connected to both the IGIGI (Watchers) and to
ISHTAR]. That no evil shall drawn near I set AMEL-DISPU
and LAT-ARAG as ["guardians," "wards"] of the doorway,
with HULDUPPU to banish the existing evils. Within the

---

4   *Usurtu*—the "*mandala*" or "magick circle" of operations.

door I have charged the twin warriors of "lime"—and the Watchers shall guard the door on the right and on the left."

The Prerequisites:
...to be performed by the "Pure Offspring of the Deep" (meaning the abode of EA-ENKI)—else, the Sons (Race) of Marduk.
...eat what is good and drink what is sweet—allow nothing "evil" to drawn near against your watching. [This portion may have been a part of some incantation being directed to a "guardian spirit," not necessarily the priest.]

The Incantation:
...is the Incantation of MARDUK.[5]

The Magician:
...is the embodiment of MARDUK, N son of N, whose god is N. and whose goddess is N, (in whose body the "sickness" lies).

The Performance:
...the incantation is spoken when the cattle come home and when the cattle go out.

THE MAQLU BURNINGS REVISITED

The words KAS.SA.PI and KAS.SAP.TI appear often in the Banishing and Exorcism tablets of Mesopotamia. The most common used transliteration of the Maqlu Tablets also uses the expressions "*lukassapi*" and "*kassapti*" (e.g. "*lukassapi u kassapti*").[6]

The name GIRRA appears frequently and is generally interpreted as a spiritual sentient entity unto itself. It may be that the literal "fire god" is GIBIL (and also NUSKU), but the expression of "GIRRA" could be more accurately translated as "fires of god"—as in the fires that a "god would wield" themselves. This could be very critical in reconstructing the tradition, changing implications of many lines found in the Maklu (or *Maqlu*) Tablets.

---

5   Also known as the "*Incantation of Eridu*" or "*Incantation of the Deep (EA)*."
6   *Lukassapi u kassapti*—"the evil sorcerer and evil sorceress."

For example, the line given: GIRRA su.ta.bil.su.nu.ti[7]
Might not be literally: "Fire-God carry them away."
It could be interpreted as: "Fires of God, carry them away."

Another example from the M-Tablet series: the Babylonian "In-cantation Against the Ancient Ones and Their Worshipers"—where it is translated originally:—

"GIRRA, Lord of the Flames sears and burns you to the core."

In the above passage, the tablet says "Lord of the Flames" only because the name GIRRA is translated traditionally and added for clarification. But the description given in the remaining lines calls the same power forth as "Flames of the Lord."

104. EN *dgirra a.ri.ru mar da.nim qar.du*
     Flaming Spirit GIRRA, Fires born of ANU
105. *iz.zu ahemes.su at.ta*
     Fiercest among your brethren
106. *sa ki.ma NANNA-SIN u dsamas ta.da.an.nu di.i.nu*
     Bring the Judgment of NANNA and SAMAS
107. *di.i.ni di.ni puruss.ai purusus*
     Be the Jury of my case—The Judge of the Decision
108. *qu.mi kas.sa.pi u kas.sap.ti*
     Burn the ("my") evil sorcerer and evil sorceress
109. *dgirra qu.mu lukassapi u fkassapti*
     GIRRA, burn the evil sorcerer and evil sorceress
110. *dgirra qu.li lukassapi u fkassapti*
     GIRRA, consume the evil sorcerer and sorceress
111. *dgirra qu.mi.su.nu.ti*
     GIRRA, burn them now!
112. *dgirra qu.li.su.nu.ti*
     GIRRA, consume them now!
113. *dgirra ku.su.us.su.nu.ti*
     GIRRA, overpower ["overwhelm"] them now!
114. *dgirra a.ru.uh.su.nu.ti*
     GIRRA, destroy ["annihilate"] them now!
115. *dgirra su.ta.bil.su.nu.ti*
     GIRRA, carry them away immediately!

---

7   *Maqlu Tablet II, line 115.*

Maqlu cuneiform tablets are used by priests to counter actions made by "wicked magick-users," especially when they have made a specific person their target. The intention of these rites is clear: to appeal to Higher Powers of the pantheon, which is same source of universal energy as the Evil Sorcerer's magic. The priest cuts them off from their source by a pious appeal to the ANUNNAKI, and finally the "belittlement" or "dispersal" of their disharmonious energies, "washed away in waters" or, as can be seen often in the Burning Rites, "incineration by fire."

In Babylon and among the Mardukite cult, mystical objects would be used by priests for ceremonies of offering (appeasing the gods) and healing sickness or curses (petition to the gods). These objects often bore the names of deities, especially the Supernal Trinity of ANU, ENLIL and ENKI. In addition to the Mardukite sevenfold *zonei* of the Babylonian system, the ancients Sumerians adhered to a different "Ninurtian"[8] hierarchy prior to (and concurrent with) the sealing of the Younger ANUNNAKI powers by MARDUK. Historians refer to them as the "Seven Ninurtas" (translated "A.DAD" in some systems). They are:—

1. URA'S of Dilba
2. NINURTA of Nippur
3. ZABABA of Ki's(h)
4. NABU of Borsippa
5. NERGAL of Kutha
6. MARDUK of Babylon
7. PABILSAG of Isin

Afflictions of the people were recognized by priests as a "spiritual entity" or "daemon"—whether or not they are self-induced (by obsession or uncleanliness) or brought on by another (the "wicked" person). It may be that this belief makes "exorcising" of sickness easier from a mystical perspective (e.g. "sympathetic magic"). While the true function of "spiritual atonement" may have been threshed out of "western religion"—it would seem that the practice of this is not only vital for "curing" but essential for the regular maintenance of well-being.

Combative magick seems wholly "fire oriented" when immolating the wickedness that has been "sent to" a target. But what of

8   NINURTA—the official heir-son of ENLIL.

the poor soul who has become the victim of a different "curse" or "illness," one fated by the "gods" whereby some social or cleanliness taboo has been broken. For this we have "atonement"—which carries a root meaning: "to wash away," therefore removing the sickness that has been "summoned to" a being, knowingly or not. In fact, the "Surpu" Tablet series[9] carries with it a considerable list of "sins" or "taboos" that a person may have committed by accident, thus resulting in "casual" illness or affliction.

Considering many of the ancient taboos: unclean sexual relations (with animals), drinking water from a poor source or coming into contact with an environment or person that may be a contagion for disease, it makes good sense that physical and observable consequences of these things would lead to a belief in "sin" (also the Babylonian name for NANNA) and "divine curses" (retribution) for such actions.

Curiously, a charm from the Surpu Tablets (Akkadian) actually appear in the forefront for rites of the AA or Argentum Astrum in the instructions for "Casting the Circle":—

Ban! Ban! Ban!
Barrier that none shall pass!
Barrier of the Gods, that none may break!
Barrier of Heaven and Earth,
The Bond unchangeable.
That no god may amend,
And no god or man shall break free.

For the closing, the Egyptian form of MA.AT [Word of Truth, Word of Power] is evoked as a means of *clearing*:—

IPSOS
Breath of the Universe, Soul of the Realm.
MAAT – speak the Word of Truth (east)
MAAT – share the Light of Justice (south)
MAAT – lead the Way of Balance (west)
MAAT – heal the Order of the Realm (north)
MAAT – above me (heights)

---

9   Portions of which appear within this present *Tablet-H* cycle of material.

MAAT – below me (depths)
MAAT – embracing ["encompassing"] all things (center).
Come Forth and be the Fire in my Heart.
Come Forth and be the Life of my Future.
Come Forth and let the Magical Child be born.
ABRAHADABRA

Finally, the continuation of the first charm is as follows:—

A snare ["net"] without escape, set for "evil"
A net which none can control to spread evil.
Whether it be the evil genius, daemon or ghost,
Or the evil devil, evil god or evil fiend,
Or hag-demon, ghoul, or thieving-sprite,
Or wraith, nightmare, or mistress of the night,
Or evil plague, fever-sickness, or unclean disease.
Whatsoever has attacked the shining waters of ENKI,
May the "net" of ENKI capture it;
Or whatsoever has spoiled the grains of NISABA,
May the "net" of NISABA combat it;
Or whatsoever has broken the sacred barrier,
Let the barrier of the gods be protected,
And the bond of heaven and earth, be free.
That which does not reverence the Elder Gods,
May the great gods trap it,
May the great gods curse it;
Whatsoever has attacked the house,
May the great gods cast it into an enclosure;
Or whatsoever swirls circles round and round to confuse,
May the great gods cast it into a place with no escape;
Or whatsoever the gets closed into the house by the door,
May the great gods cast it into a house with no exit;
Or whatsoever slips past the bolted door,
May the great gods ever keep hold over it with a bolt.
That which blows into the household at the crevices,
Or that which forces its way through the latch,
Like the waters may it pour out from that place,
Like a glass cup may it be thrashed into pieces,
Like a delicate tile may it be broken so easily.
Or whatsoever makes its way over the wall,
May the great gods cut off its wings;

Or whatsoever finds a way to hide in the rooms,
May the great gods cut its throat;
Or whatsoever sneaks to steal a glance of the rooms,
May the great gods force out its eyes;
Or whatsoever mutters curses quietly in the dwelling,
May the great gods force its mouth shut forever;
Or whatsoever roams free in the attics,
May the great gods conceal it in the "between";
Or whatsoever darkens the dawn,
May the great gods imprison it in the "place of sunrise."

MARDUKITE MEDICINE, CURSES & ATTONEMENT

As has been expressed implicitly throughout Mardukite literature, the role of MARDUK in Babylon and Egypt was to surpass primitive religions (including those pretending to be monotheistic) dedicated to other ANUNNAKI that sought to enslave mankind, keeping them removed in ignorance from the Source in a Realm of Darkness. Much of it originated not of blatantly malignant expressions, but necessity. MARDUK is unique in his position among the "gods" in that he has the power (granted by the "fifty names") to supersede them and their decisions in the Material Realm. We see evidence for this again in the "Surpu" tablets which lists "sins" or "taboos" as MAM.IT. In one part we find:—

The MAMIT of any kind that afflicts a man,
MARDUK, Priest of the Gods, can attend.

We translate it to literally apply to sickness specifically, choosing the words "afflict" and "attend." An alternative would be to liken the situation to a curse placed on the person for violating some MAMIT, thus replacing these two words with "binding" and "loosen." Several lines of the third tablet of the *Surpu Series* are spent in listing the deities whose powers MARDUK can actual undo:—

MARDUK can loosen the MAMIT of ANU and ANTU, BEL [ENLIL] and BELIT [NINLIL], ENKI and DAMKINA, NANNA and NINGAL, SAMAS and AYA, ADAD and SALA, NABU and TASMIT, NINIB...

It continues throughout the entire pantheon! In addition, MAR-
DUK is hailed *"musim simate sa ilani kalama"*—the one who
determines [holds] the fates [destiny?] of the gods, though some
scholars believe this role to be purely cyclic (connected to the
zodiacal ages), or revolving among the ANUNNAKI—the Mardukite lore would suggest otherwise—that the Younger God
gained immediate respect among his Elders by doing "what you
ANUNNAKI could not have."

On an Assyrian tablet used for healing, the god SAMAS is evoked
as "Chief of the Gods." Scholarly examination reveals that
SAMAS is AZAZEL—a being also connected to the Wild Goat God
of the Woods (ENKI), for too, consider Leviticus in the Old Testament, where Aaron "casts lots" upon two goats, one for the Lord
(BEL) and one for AZAZEL (SAMAS). The goat selected by the
Lord is sacrificed as a sin offering–but the goat to SAMAS is to be
presented while still living to the Lord, "to make atonement
over it" and then it is set free into the wilderness (apparently
the wild domain of AZAZEL). AZAZEL (SAMAS) appears frequently in Judeo-Christian scriptures in relation to the *"Day of
Atonement."* The Assyrian Tablet reads:—

> By the MAAT [power word of truth] of ENKI
> May this man, the son of his god N.,
> Become pure, clean and bright among things.
> May this man be cleansed like a vessel of fat [lard, oil],
> May this man be cleansed like a vessel of butter, &tc.
> Unto SAMAS, Chief of the Gods, commend him,
> By SAMAS, Chief of the Gods,
> May this man's welfare be protected [secured, sealed]
> By the hands of the ANUNNAKI ["gods"].

These appeals to the "Higher," are similar in nature and intent
to the actual Hebrew prayer that accompanies the goat-atone-
ment rite—it should be clear that ENLIL is actually thought to be
the wrathful Lord of the Old Testament Hebrew:—

> Lord, I have acted iniquitously,
> I have trespassed and sinned before You;
> I, my household, and the sons of Aaron,
> Your holy [sacred, good] race.

O Lord, forgive the iniquities,
Forgive the transgressions and sins that
I, my household, and the sons of Aaron,
The holy people dedicated to You,
As is written in the law of Moses, Your servant:
"On this day He will forgive you,
To cleanse you from all your sins before the Lord;
Ye shall be clean."

According to writings found in the *Book of Enoch*, AZAZEL is the Chief of the Grigori, another word for "fallen angels." The modern Semitic version leaves us with the impression that this being is a generic "*Satan.*" The "warrior" nature is what is actually called upon by MARDUK in the construction of the weapons used to kill KINGU and TIAMAT.[10] In the Book of Enoch, after the "Sons of God" fall and then interbreed with the "Daughters of Men":—

AZAZEL taught men to make swords, knives, shields and breastplates and made known to the people the natures of the earthly metals and the art of working them properly; and the natures of bracelets and ornamentation of the body and the beautification of the eyes and face; with all manners of precious stones and coloring tinctures. And there arose much godlessness in the hearts of the people, for they had become vain with their knowledge and committed acts of fornication now being that they were led astray had they easily become completely corrupted in their ways.

The physical (apparent) impact of MARDUK dissolves into the "unseen" with the passage of time—all but to be forgotten—as the "Sun-King" or "Sun-God"—a warrior spirit among the gods—makes a centralized appearance. Keeping in mind the words, "God", "Heaven", "Planet" and "Star" are essentially synonymous in the Mesopotamian paradigms, we can see how some of these concepts are confused today, thousands of years later.

In the following rite, a dead man is to be buried in the ground—all of his personal affects are to be washed (cleansed with water)

---

10 In the Babylonian "Epic of Creation"—*Enuma Elis.*

—and a figure is made in his image to also be buried so as not to incite the visitation of his spirit thereafter. The burial hymn is dedicated to SAMAS or an equivalent solar-god name:—

> SAMAS, King of Heaven and Earth,
> Judge of what is Above and Below,
> Lord of the Dead – Ruler of the Living.
> SAMAS, the Dead have risen and appeared,
> The "*edimmu*"[11] of my father and mother,
> The "*edimmu*" of my brother or my sister,
> Let them accept the worldly death and be free.

DEVILS & DEMONS OF BABYLON
(FEVERS, EVIL SPIRITS & HEADACHES)

In the first decades of the 20th Century, many ancient tablets came to public attention, translated from their original cuneiform by some extraordinary and adventurous minds—most of them not even realizing what part they were playing as the Gates began to crack open. At the same time, the magic of Hebrews, Sumerians, Babylonians, Akkadians and Assyrians began to earn publication for public exploration. Now—for a century, few but the elite have even dared explore the mysteries, shrouding it in gloom, dangers and fears innumerably connected to the same horrifying images of cthonic gore. Darkness is always requiring Holy Magic to bind it as seen in further examples of these most ancient explorations.

◊ ◊ ◊   ◊ ◊ ◊   ◊ ◊ ◊

Using the hair of a "virgin child", a "wise woman" must spin it "double" [twice thick] to make a rope. Bind twice seven [fourteen] knots. Perform the "*Incantation of Eridu*" and then:—

> Bind the head of the sick man. Bind the neck of the sick man. Bind the life of the sick man. Bind the limbs of the sick man.

Encircle the couch [bed, etc.] the man lays in with the "Waters of the Incantation" ["holy water," water blessed by the priest's

---

11 *Edimmu*—traditionally translated as "ghost" or "ancestral spirit."

incantations prior]—and may the head... ...scend to heaven as
the smoke of the incense ... ...nd like the waters
that rain down on the lan... ...ne be seeped deep
in the "beneath"—returnin... ...d in which it was
born. The incantation of fi... ...amen, "it is fin-
ished" or "so mote it be") us... ...rites:—

ZI DINGIR ANNA [ANU] KA...
By the Heavens you are exc... ...e] it!
ZI DINGIR KIA KANPA
By the Earth you are exorcis...
BAN BAN BAN
By the Gods I conjure an imp...
By the Heavens I conjure an i... ...e blockade!
By the Earth I conjure an impassable bridge!
By the Heavens and Earth, Powers of Light and Darkness,
I conjure the binding that none shall break!
No God shall annul; No man shall change!
A net without escape; which cannot be used for evil.

[restored ending to the prayer of finality]

Amat EA *lisu dingir damgal nunna heensidi* [...]
May the word [MAAT] of ENKI make clear [passage
   for me],
DAMKINA *liste y sir dingir silig elim nun na dusag
   zuabge sagga tagtaglibi zaakan,*
May DAMKINA guide us with the light of the Truth,
   and the Eldest Son of the Deep,
MARDUK *m-dru r-tsiuu sa apsii buunnuu duummiiku*
MARDUK, thine is the power to brighten and bless.

◊ ◊ ◊   ◊ ◊ ◊   ◊ ◊ ◊

An evil spirit is prevalent in the land.
It torments the people both above and below.
It is a pestilence, a plague with no rest.
It wishes desolation for all wherever it goes.
The Great Demon—The Great Spirit—The Great Fiend
That which roams where the multitudes gather.
The angry fierce quaking storm that thrashes about.

Like the pestilence in the streets,
Which NERGAL had brought.
It is not I, but MARDUK who performs the incantations.

CAUSES OF HEADACHE, DISEASE & POSSESSION
[According to the "Surpu" Tablet Series]

The person who has...
   ...sinned against his God.
   ...sinned against his Goddess.
   ...performed the unknown sin against his God.
   ...performed the unknown sin against his Goddess.
   ...misconducted himself before the God.
   ...misconducted himself before the Goddess.
   ...made his God and Goddess angry with him.
   ...sought undue secrets of the Gods of Heaven.
   ...sought undue secrets of the Temple-Shrines of Earth.
   ...slighted what is due to the Gods.
   ...sought undue favor of the Gods at the Temple-Shrines.
   ...offered impure sacrifice at the Altar of Offering.
   ...offered sacrifice to the [Gods] and taken it back.
   ...destroyed the sacrifice made at the Altar of Offering.
   ...obstructed the sacrifices made by another.
   ...caused obstruction between [friends, family].
   ...eaten the flesh of a sacrifice at the Altars of Offering.
   ...held hatred towards an elder.
   ...shed his neighbor's blood.
   ...propositioned their neighbor's wife.
   ...propositioned their neighbor's husband.
   ...used a false balance in business affairs.
   ...removed or misplaced a boundary or landmark.
   ...unjustly entered their neighbor's house.
   ...taken their neighbor's garment.
   ...stolen or caused another to steal.
   ...said "no" for "yes" and "yes" for "no" [lying].
   ...been straight in the mouth but not true in the heart.
   ...promised pleasure and joy but not given it.
   ...spoken of what is unholy.
   ...spoken wickedness.

...caused a judge to receive a bribe.
...wronged his city.
...opposed one in authority under MARDUK.
...give in small things but refused in great.
...transgressed the righteous.
...offended the righteous.
...set their hand to evil acts.
...set their hearts to follow after evil.
...stopped a neighbor's canal [water supply].
...been banned of weapons but seeks them.
...set his hand to evil sorceries and witchcraft.
...pointed at the holy fire.
...taken a prolonged seat in the sun [sun-stroke].
...struck the young of an animal.
...tearing up plants in the desert.
...tearing of plants and trees.
...raised a fire and falsely sworn by a god.
...has tasted from the unclean cup.
...has tasted from the unclean plate.
...has tasted from the unclean dish.

THE BOOK OF AL-JILWAH
& MELEK TA'US
(Tablet-J)

Few occultists who remain in the Light are probably privy to lore of the ancient Yezidi sect. The Yezidi follow a tradition ded-icated to the "God of the Black Mountain" who gave to them wisdom in what is known as the oldest of the *"Black Books."* While the Realm of Light has shied away from such—or believed they have attained more than a glimpse of it in their *"Books of Shadows,"* it is this Divine Encounter that has been omitted from traditional biblical tales for its connections and devotion to the Darkness.

The Yezidi are a uniquely distinct genetic Mesopotamian sect that still resides in Northern Iraq[12] and can trace bloodlines and traditions to the ancient ANUNNAKI directly. They practice a unique form of Mardukite Monotheism under the guise of a messenger named Melek Ta'us, similar to the manifestation of MARDUK as Mithras and Mazda—as *One*—in the Zoroastrian schema.[13] This same current of energy is also manifest as Maitreya for Buddhists.

Yezidis claim to share Adamic (from "Adam") descent but not of Eve. Their lore suggests that the remaining global population outside of their sect is also outside of this "special" lineage. And to them, they were given "Revelation" *("Al-Jilwah")* from their Divine Encounters with a being who the Judeo-Christians de-noted as *Satan* (and perhaps others might liken to ENKI).

---

12 Among other travesties of the Mardukite/Anunnaki Legacy, the Islamic "ISIS" terrorists targeted the modern Yezidi people for genocide.
13 Noted in the *"Tablet-Z"* series in *"Necronomicon: The Anunnaki Bible."*

According to Yezidic Tradition, there is an All-Father or YAZDAN who created the Seven ANUNNAKI ("emissaries" or "angels") including Azazel (or Azazil). The word "Azif" and the actual book, "Al Azif," is a Yezidic tome detailing the lore, or literally "howls" of the Djinns (or jinn). Some scholars of the *Necronomicon*-Cycle will note that one of the popular Arabic translations for the title of the work is, in fact, *Al Azif*.[14] The association with the "buzzing of insects" could be meant to mean both the "swarm" and the "sound," furthering the connection of the *Outer Ones* with "UFO" extraterrestrial beings.

The seven deities or "Great Gods" created by YAZDAN are connected to, as we might expect, both the seven-star constellation of Ursa Major—*the Great Bear*—but also the seven visible "stars" (planets) of the ancient world, that of the ANUNNAKI Celestial *Zonei*. Chaldean lore suggests origins of the zodiacal wheel as a chart for shifting ages of rulership among the twelve-fold ANUNNAKI of the "Older Pantheon" (of "Elder Gods"). The sevenfold schema of the "Younger Pantheon" is dominant during the Babylonian era. Yezidic lore suggests that each of these seven figures is given reign of the material kingdom in turn, marked by an age of 10,000 years (in their reckoning).

QU'RET AL-YEZID – REVELATIONS OF MELEK-TA'US

My knowledge encompasses the very Truth of all that Is,
And My wisdom is not separated from My Source,
The Manifestation of My [*blood*] descent is clear unto you,
And when it is Revealed to the Children of Adam it will
   become as a Sword of Fire among the multitudes,
And many will tremble thereby.

All habitations (especially the desert spaces) are of
My own creation, programs I have set into action,
All completely from within My own strength,
And not the result of the false gods;
Wherefore I am He that men should rightly worship,
Not the false gods of their books, wrongly written;
Poorly remembered.

---

14 Also named for the sound of the "buzzing of insects."

But they come to know Me, a Peacock of bronze and of gold,
My Wings spread over the [*Kaba*] Temple and Church,
   not to be overshadowed.
And in the secret cave of My wisdom it is known:
I am the Voice of God; there is no God but Myself,
An Archangel commanding legions, Melek Ta'us.

Knowing this, who would dare deny Me?
Knowing this, who would dare fail to worship Me?
Knowing this, who would dare to continue the
   worship of false idols found in the Koran and Bible?
Knowing this, who shall make that effort to no ends?

But know this: that he who knows Me,
I may cast into pleasure-filled gardens of Paradise!
But the Yezid who chooses to not know Me,
I will make death, as life, one-thousand afflictions.

Proclaim then, I am the only Archangel to be exalted;
And I will make prosperous whom I wish to rest my Eye,
And I will enliven those I choose to rest my Hand.
Proclaim then, I alone am to be praised of the
Seven Towers [*Pillars*] of the ANUNNAKI,
My Name shall be heard from the Mountain of Ararat to
   the Western Sea.
Proclaim then, Let the Light of True Knowledge flash
   forth from the Ziarahs [*Seraphim, Zonei or Satans*],
Flash forth from the rivers of the Euphrates
And the Tigris [the boundaries of Mesopotamia] to the hidden
   folds of Shambalah.

Let My Kingdom be carried from its safe place into the Temple,
And let the Yezidi know Me by My Manifestations,
Even Sheikan, Sinjar, Haliteyeh, Malliyeh, and Lepcho,
   [*a series of esoteric proper names are given*]
And the Kotchar [another obscure name] who wander
   among the heathens [*savage unsaved multitudes*].

MESHAF I-RESH – BLACK BOOK OF MELEK-TA'US

In the beginning was the Invisible One [God]
Who brought forth the White Pearl,
From out of His own precious Essence.

He then brought forth a bird into being named Anfar.
And on its back He placed the White Pearl,
And there it rested for forty thousand years.

Then, on the first day, Sunday,
He created an Archangel over all angels [sky-gods]
Named 'Ezrail', which is Melek Ta'us, the Peacock Angel,
The First-to-Be, the chief of all.

Each subsequent day, an angel to serve Melek Ta'us.
On Monday, Dardael came forth, who is Sheikh Hasan.
On Tuesday Izrasel came forth, who is Sheikh Shams.
On Wednesday, Jibrael [Gabriel—GIBIL] came forth,
   who is Sheikh Abu-Bekr [AIQ-BKR]
On Thursday, Azrael, who is Sajadin, came forth.
On Friday, Shemnael came forth, who is Nassurud-Din.
On Saturday Nurael, who is Zuriel, came forth.
Melek Ta'us was chief over them all.

When after all this had been done,
The Invisible One [God] returned to its abode,
   and acted no more.
From this point, Melek Ta'us was left to act alone.

First he moved to separate the heavens by seven [Zonei],
And also a veil for the earth, sun, and moon.
Seeing the barrenness of the realms,
He created humans, animals, various birds and beasts,
Placing them in the between spaces accompanied by angels.
Melek Ta'us stood before the White Pearl and shouted.
It was broken into four pieces.
He commanded Gabriel to take two of the pieces;
One was placed beneath the earth,
   and the other was placed at the Gate of Heaven.

The other two pieces were placed in the sun and the moon,
And the stars were created from their fragments,

Suspended in heaven for the delight of the [gods].

The Mighty Lord Melek Ta'us spoke:
"O angel brethren, I will to create the Adam and Eve,
And I will make them human beings, and from them,
   two shall arise, out of the loins of Adam, Shehr ibn Jebr;
   and from him shall arise a single people on the earth:
The Yezidi people."

Then Melek Ta'us commanded Gabriel to come forth
And take parts from the four corners of the world:
   the elements: earth, air, fire and water.
He man from the four and instilled a fragment of
   Divine Spark in each, a "soul" given by his power.

Gabriel was commanded to place Adam in
   the Gardens of Paradise [E.DIN],
Where he was permitted to eat fruit of every green herb,
Only wheat was he commanded not to eat.

After a hundred years Ta'us Melek went to God asking:
"How shall Adam increase and multiply,
   and where are his offspring?"
God replied to him: "This is not my concern.
   Into your hands I have given it."
Melek Ta'us then asked of Adam: "Have you eaten the wheat?"
And Adam answered: "No, I am forbidden to do so."
Melek Ta'us then said to him:
   "It would behoove you to eat of the wheat."
So, Adam ate of the wheat.
But, after he had eaten, his stomach swelled up.
Ta'us Melek drove him out of Paradise [E.DIN],
   left him alone, and ascended into the heavens disgusted.

Adam suffered from the pains in his stomach,
   because his waste had no outlet.
God blessed Adam by sending a bird,
Which helped him by making an outlet for Adam's relief.
(Though some say the bird was Gabriel transformed.)
Eve was then created from beneath Adam's left arm-pit.

Melek Ta'us descended to the earth,
Returning for the sake of our people [the Yezidis]

And he brought kings to rule alongside the ancient kings
  (of the Assyrians);
Nesrukh, who is Nassurud-Din [*Nasiru'd-Din*] and
Kamush, who is King Fakhru'd-Din and Artimus,
  who is King Shamsu'd-Din.

And when after these had ruled, we had two kings,
The first and second Persian *Shapurs,*
Who are *Mazdayasnians* of AHURA-MAZDA,
And whose rule was given to last one hundred and fifty years.
From this tree has brought us the seed of our Amirs[15]
Through to the present day; And we in turn became divided.

Know that it is not permitted to utter the name SHAITAN
  —because it is the name of God.
Nor should any name be spoken that resembles this,
Such as Kitan, Sharr and Shatt;
Nor also any vocalization resembling Malun, Malek or Nayl.

In the time before the Common Era,
Our religion was called idol-worship:
  and the Jews, Christians, Muslims and Persians
  steered clear from our traditions.

King Ahab and Amran were among our own,
  and they have named the God of Ahab, BEELZEBUB,
  whom they have also called among us, Pirbub.
We had a king from among our own in BABYLON;
  whose name was Bukhti-Nossor [*Nebuchadnezzer*],
And Ahasuerus in Persia was among our own,
And in Constantinople, Aghriqalus was among our own.

◊ ◊ ◊   ◊ ◊ ◊   ◊ ◊ ◊

Know too the secret:
When first before heaven and earth had been made,
The Lord was suspended over the waters,
In a chariot above the waters, He was suspended.

Then the Lord ascended into the heavens,
And the heavens were condensed for His existence

---

15 AMAR—or "Chieftain Ruler."

And fixed the heavens to exist without supports.
Then the earth was condensed and sealed away from it.
From His own Divine Essence [*sparks of light*],
He created the six [*gods*] to be like the light of a lamp,
Each successively lighting off the light of the other.

And he said to the first: "Ascend!
And create something else apart from you."
And the Moon [*Gate-Zonei*] came into being,
   and so began the succession of the Spheres [*gods*].

KITAB AL-JILWAH – THE SERMON OF REVELATION

This is the Book of Al-Jilwah recording a true and faithful communication from the God, *Melek Ta'us*. He has sent his servant
messenger into this world to guide and separate his chosen
people from their errors [sins]. The texts which follow are the
account first made to the faithful servants via an oral tradition—
but the Lord allowed the book of *Al-Jilwah* to be written before
him, so long as no strangers to the Yezidi would behold it.

* * *

1. I was, and am now, and will continue unto eternity, ruling
over all creatures and ordering the affairs and deeds of those
who are under my command. [*Omnipotence*]

2. I am presently available to those who trust in me and call
upon me in time of need, neither is there any place void of me
where I am not capable of presence. [*Omnipresence*]

3. I am involved in the natures of all those things which
strangers call evil only because they are not according to their
own desire. [*Freedom – Civil Disobedience*]

4. Every Aeon [age] has a Ruler [regent who is under my counsel
– Every generation changes their natures by the Chief [Lord] of
this World, so that each one of them has his turn and cycle to
fulfill his charge. [*Zodiacal Age*]

5. I grant indulgences freely but according to the merits of those
qualities which is laden in the disposition of the nature. [*Karmic
Law of Returns*]

6. He who opposes me shall experience grievous regret.

7. No other gods may interfere in my business and work: whatsoever I determine, that is what will be.

8. The Scriptures which are in the hands of strangers, even though they were written by prophets and apostles, others have turned the truth of these aside, and rebelled, and perverted them; and each one of them confuses the other and all are lost to it.

9. Truth and Falsehood are distinguished by proving them at the time of their inception.

10. I will fulfill my promise to those who put their trust in me, those will uphold the covenant of the Ancient of Days, and also to those who act contrary to it, by accordance of the judgment made by the wise or my Rulers [Regents] that I delegate to execute my authority for me while on earth.

11. I take notes of all affairs, and promote the performance of what is deemed useful [good] in its due time.

12. I direct and teach those who will actually follow my teaching, who find with me joy and delight by natural accord far greater than any worldly joy.

13. I choose to reward and punish the progeny of Adam by all different manners of which I have knowledge.

14. I hold in my hand the means to control the earth and what is above and below it.

15. I do not concern myself much with the other races, but neither do I withhold good from them; much less do I begrudge it to those who are my chosen people and obedient servants to hold prejudice.

16. I will surrender active worldly control into the hands of those proven, in accordance with my will, to be friends in some shape and fashion to such as they are faithful and abide by my counsel.

17. Indeed, I take and I give; I can make rich and I can make poor; happy and wretched, all in accordance to the natural environments and seasons [*cycles*], of which there are none who have the right to interfere, or to withdraw man from the system I control.

18. I bring down pain and sickness upon those who strive to thwart me.

19. He who is recorded as mine shall not experience death like other men.

20. I deem that no man should dwell in this lower world for more than the period prescribed by me; and, if I wish it, I will send him back into this world a second and a third time (or more) by way of the transmigration of the soul, and such exists by a universal law.

21. I guide you without a scripture to be profaned and point to you the way by an unseen hand, though my friends and such will recognize me in my teachings and can be found by their observation of the precepts, which is not a laborious accord and will adapt itself to time and cultures as needed.

22. I punish those who do not adhere to the laws also in other worlds.

23. The children of Adam don't know the Secrets of Destiny [*Fate, Union*] and so they fall to error in their beliefs and followed actions.

24. I control the beasts of the field and the birds of the heaven and the fish of the sea, as all of them are in my hand.

25. All of the secret treasures and wondrous hoards buried deep in the heart of the earth are known to me, and I can cause one after another to inherit these riches on earth.

26. I make visible [*manifest*] my signs and wonders [*miracles*] to those who will receive them and self-honestly seek them from me in their due season [*time, cycle*].

27. The opposition of strangers to me and my followers do nothing except injure my cause—and know that they will be dealt with as is deserving.

28. The ordering of the spheres [*heavens, worlds*], the revolution of Aeons [*ages, cycles*], and the changing of their Rulers [*Regents*] are mine from eternity [*Kingship has descended from Heaven*].

29. Those who are not capable of reaching their appointed Destiny [*Fate, Union*], him I will chastise in my time [*age, Aeon*] and will cause him to relive his former charge.

30. The seasons of the Material Kingdom are four, and the elements are four; these have I maintained to secure the needs of my creatures.

31. The scriptures of strangers are accepted by me in so far as they accord and agree with my ordinances and do not contradict them; for they have been for the most part corrupted by mortal minds.

32. There are Three who are opposed to me, and these three names I hate above all else, and I shall not reveal [*possibly the Supernal Trinity of the ANUNNAKI*].

33. My promises are fulfilled to those who keep to the law.

34. Those who have undergone tribulations as martyrs for my sake will be compensated without fail in one of the worlds [spheres, heavens] in my domain.

35. It is my desire that all of my followers are united together on account that there are multitudes who are strangers to them and may band in opposition.

36. Those observing my law should reject teachings and dogma that are not from me.

37. Do not make mention of my name or my attributes [natures], as idle strangers do, or else be guilty of a sin by an ethic for which you have no knowledge of.

38. Honor my symbol and image, let the mark of it remind you of our covenant and of what has been neglected of my laws and ordinances.

39. Be obedient and attentive to my servants who are blessed by my Eye and Hand; listen to what they communicate to you of that knowledge of from the unseen which they have receive from me.

144

THE BOOK OF QLIPPOTH
& THE OTHER SIDE
(Tablet-Q)

The close of the Year-1 cycle of Mardukite materials [indicating *Liber 9*][16] is meant to bridge what is in the "light" to what is laying hidden in the "shadows," in the "darkness," in the "night." O, Sons of the Night, gather around to hear the words which might bring you to the "Crossing to the Abyss"[17]—that which you desire must strongly in your heart—your heart's desire.

◊ ◊ ◊   ◊ ◊ ◊   ◊ ◊ ◊

The evil [fever] has set upon like a deluge,
Wide and broad it fills the whole of the Earth.
Enveloped in Terror, cloaked in Fear;
It roams freely about the streets...
It invisibly stands beside any man...
It sits and whispers to any man...
When it enters the home, its appearance is unknown.
When it goes forth out of the home,
It has gone unnoticed ["is not perceived"].

THE BROKEN FRAGMENT

It has been established, the Nations shall return to the Source.
Nations of men will return to the Womb of Creation.
To NIBIRU, Eternal Creatrix—Mother Goddess.
The ANUNNAKI have set forth the decree.

---

16 The "Tablet-Q" series (along with "Tablet-H" and "Tablet-J") first appeared in "*Liber 9*," the final installment of the original Mardukite work released in 2009 and eventually compiled into "*Necronomicon: The Anunnaki Bible.*"

17 *Crossing to the Abyss*—the original label phrase for Year-2 Mardukite Chamberlains work culminated in the titles: "*Sumerian Religion*" (Liber 50), "*Necronomicon Revelations*" (Liber R) and "*Babylonian Magic*" (Liber 51).

From Heaven, the ANUNNAKI decree the fates for their creation.
From ANU is ENKI and ENLIL
From ENKI and ENLIL and NINHURSAG
Came the race to relieve the toil of the IGIGI [Watchers].

ENKI [PTAH], Founder of Men,
Founder of the Temple-Shrine in ERIDU,
ANU—Father of All.
Father of the Dynasty in BAD-TIBIRA,
Father of the Dynasty in LARSA,
Father of the Dynasty in SIPPAR and SHURUPAK.

Aye, the First Cities of Men,
Were founded by the ANUNNAKI,
Those who fell to the Earth from the Heavens,
They were the Light-Bearers among the Nations,
They were men of renown, revered among the Nations.

ANU, ENLIL, ENKI—Sent Messengers.
Multitudes poured forth from the Heavens [IGIGI, etc.]
Then, led by MARDUK – all evil was expelled.
The Divine Ordinances of the Temple-Shrines,
The Books of Knowledge and Rites,
These were entrusted to the priest-kings of men...

MARDUK & THE PLAGUE

May MARDUK, Eldest Son of ERIDU
Sprinkle the afflicted one with pure water,
Clean water – Bright water;
With the water, twice seven times,
That he may be pure, that he may be clean;
Let the evil RABISU Daemon go forth
And stand away from the afflicted one;
May a kindly SEDU [spirit],
May a kindly LAMASSU [guardian],
Come forth and be present near his body.

The priest is to make an image of the affected person in dough,
so as to force the Plague-God that afflicts the person to come
away from the body and into the image. Ancient tablets list the

Plague-God as NAMTARU, and in other places it may be found as URA. The texts continue:—

Plague-God that devours the land like fire,
Plague-God that attacks the man like a fever,
Plague-God that roams the wind like a desert,
Plague-God that seizes the man like an evil thing,
Plague-God that torments like a pestilence,
Plague-God that has no hands or feet, but wanders the Night.
Plague-God that tears the afflicted man in shreds,
That binds the body of the afflicted man,
That has decreased the strength of the afflicted man,
Like a withering plant.
At night on his bed, the afflicted one cannot sleep.
The Plague-God has affected his body.
The Plague-God has seized his loins.
The god of the afflicted one is distant,
The goddess is far from the body.
MARDUK has set his eye on the body.
MARDUK has set his hand on the body.

Pull off a piece of clay from the "deep"—fashion an image of the afflicted one's form and place it in the loins of the sick man at night. At dawn, make atonement for the body and perform the Incantation of ERIDU [Mardukite Pentagram Rite], turn his face to the west, that the evil Plague-God, the Great NAMTARU, wide with dread, which has seized the body of the afflicted one, will vanish away from him.

◊ ◊ ◊ ◊ ◊ ◊ ◊ ◊ ◊

Magic Square tablets are used as talismans in the Ancient Near East and elsewhere related to secrets of the ANUNNAKI energetic "magicks" and protections offered to the priest-kings and children of MARDUK. Some tablets are designed for hanging on a wall, particularly over doorways and thresholds (physical gates). Origins of the "Peace-Love-Unity" triad used among the Ordo Nabu Maerdechai is actually derived from such a tablet, drawn with the following words: "May the Temple-Shrine of ASSUR & MARDUK be over this house!"

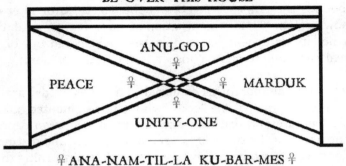

⚲ MAY THE SHRINE OF ASSUR & MARDUK ⚲
BE OVER THIS HOUSE

ANU-GOD

PEACE   MARDUK

UNITY-ONE

⚲ ANA-NAM-TIL-LA KU-BAR-MES ⚲

MARDUK went to his father for help,
To drive out the fever-daemon—
May pestilence be driven from the body.
ENKI advised him: Fashion an image of his likeness
From dough and Earth - Set it upon the ground [holy ground]
Take men with a king [noble or literal] over him,
Take his hand before the "Sun" [SAMAS].
Repeat the incantation SAR-AZAG-GA
While pouring water of his head and the Incantation of ERIDU.

THE RITUAL OF THE HANGING STONES
SHADOW RITES FROM THE UNDERWORLD
(A CTHONIC NECRONOMICON GNOSIS)

So once we have put our foot it in, all that remains is of course to dislodge the Gates. To unleash mighty forces within and around us—to bring back the ANUNNAKI so they may be established on the Earth again. And it matters not which names and ideals we attach to this ideal so long as it is maintained in the hearts and thoughts of the dedicated.

Let us discuss first the Primary Elements involved, the *primum mobium* as it were—water and air, yet also the spaces between them—the Heights and the Depths and the spaces between them. You have heard the name of Cthulhu[18]—a name that is often connected to the Crossings, to the Land of Kutha (or Cutha), to the Underworld—of the name KUTU-LU—Darkness and Shadow abounds the name of TUTU and the TUTU-LU or alter-ego [Shadow] of the TUTU[19] is what men have feared—and they know not its nature—it has simply been whispered out of the ethereal mists and remained unseen in the Realm of Light.

Know too that animal forms conjured to mind as "gods" are but shadows of the truth of the "gods" who have fragmented our beings as separate and distinct—and at first it had been decreed that the union of the two were to remain separate and distinct—the blending being taboo. This lore has existed concerning those among the Old Ones and Elder Gods that did come down to set themselves upon the "daughters of men"—though it has been written that they "corrupted" the women—we knoweth not the natures and minds of the gods.

What fierce beast waits for us at the Crossing to the Abyss—what monstrous visions will we be forced to behold? What is the nature of the Dweller at the Threshold? And in what names are we to know these by? For after climbing the Ladder of Lights and establishing the whole of the Light—what other motivation can there be except to enter into the Beyond? Perhaps one of the most fundamental of thoughts when considering the Gnosis of the *Necronomicon Cycle* is the reverberating echo of: "The Power of Man is the Power of the Ancient Ones."

◊ ◊ ◊   ◊ ◊ ◊   ◊ ◊ ◊

. . . and he read the dreaded name:
CTHULHU

. . . and he read the dreaded name:
ZKHORONZON[20]

---

18 *Cthulhu*—a name made famous by H.P. Lovecraft's fantasy-fiction writings.

19 TUTU—an alternate name for KUTU in modern high magick and ceremonial magick traditions; the name TUTU is listed as an alternate name (or title-role) for NABU, a guardian of the gates but not necessarily Cthonic.

20 "*zKhoronzon*"—in the Enochian tradition/paradigm, a name for a dragon-spirit guarding the Gate to the Outside.

◊ ◊ ◊   ◊ ◊ ◊   ◊ ◊ ◊

It has been compared to the Lovecraftian semantics—that the Depths are likened to Cthulhu and the Heights are to Yog-Sothoth. While these names, among others invoked from that mythos, do not necessarily appear one-to-one with any specific names on ancient Mesopotamian tablets or from classical mythologies. The basic planetary system (universal streams) as a Celestial Pantheon can be overlaid onto any sufficient cultural or thematic paradigm if the symbolism matches appropriate archetypal names of that mythos.

The Circle of Stone is a mystical representations of space and time, of course, *fragmented* space and *fragmented* time. The number and arrangement of the stones, just like the number of points indicated on a star. The elemental entity? The Watchtowers? Yea, they are interconnected to the Four that are One and to the Stones in the physical world raised and named to them:—

In the element of Water, Three Stones to SYTH OOLOO
In the element of Fire, Six Stones to SYTH ODOWOGG
In the element of Air, Eight Stones to HRU SYTH
In the element of Earth, Five Stones to SHUGNIGOTH

The interpretation of this, as some magical orders have arrived at, is the similarity of phonetic sounds to Lovecraftian entities— Cthulhu [SYTH OOLOO], Yog Sothoth or Ossa-dagowah [SYTH ODO-WOGG], Hastur [HRU SYTH], Shub-Niggurath [SHUG-NIG-OTH]. Then one will be intellectually inclined to draw other conclusions of formulae, such as:—

3 : Binah—Saturn: The Great Deep, Abode of KUTULU
6: Tiphareth—Sun-Fire: Solar Center, 666, YOG-SOTHOTH
8: Hod—Mercury-Air: Winged Messenger, HASTUR
5: Geburah—Mars: Goat of 1000-Young, SHUB-
                                        NIGGURATH

For those not privy to the methods of old, the ceremonial formula is simple enough: the number of stones are indicative to the energetic current being fragmented and channeled from the whole.

The circle, is as always, a holy mandala of the priest—magician representing the Universe—the inner circle may be indicative of a transitional element (e.g. the water gate or sea shells) and the measure of the diameter usually energetically reflects the current. Stones are equally spaced and "named" as they are set out or marked (much as in the manner of the shamanic Medicine Wheel)[21]—and as with any ritual, workings may be performed solely in the astral.

Lines of Power—forming "star-glyphs"—run across the surface of the most holy *nemetons* [mandala] erected as the Stones of the Ancients. They form an energetic boundary for the "circle" - they also cross the surface meeting not only the practitioner in the center, but also sharing amplified resonance with one another to aid in the building of and channeling of energetic powers. Traditionally the stones ["earth element"] are to be collected by [near] the sea ["water element"] by the light of the full moon ["lunar current"] = and the working is sealed with the Incantation of ERIDU [e.g. Mardukite Pentagram Rite].

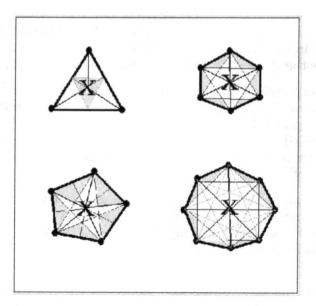

---

21 *Medicine Wheel*—see also *"The Great Magical Arcanum"* by Joshua Free.

THE LOST RITES AND LORE OF DAATH
MORE LOVECRAFTIAN NECRONOMICON GNOSIS
(SHADOWS FROM THE UNDERWORLD)

In ancient and esoteric Semitic lore, there is a hidden sphere on the tree—a transitional doorway occulted by the Light of the other Spheres—called *Daath*.[22] It is a secret unnumbered Sphere [*Sephirot*—Heaven or Gate] which is the height or summit of the material and also forms the basis and foundation (or depths) of the Supernal Triad—or Heights (whereby the "Ninth Gate" leads to the (Z)AIN). The Heights of the material realm are The Depths of the supernal Heights.

◊ ◊ ◊　◊ ◊ ◊　◊ ◊ ◊

1. AZATHOTH—The Primal Chaos, Center of Infinity, Formless, Unknown, the Anti-Thesis of Creation.
   Zodiac: Leo; Direction: Hidden South
   Alias: Azag-Thoth; Time Threshold: Sunday
   Mardukite Pantheon: SAMAS (SHAMMASH-UTU)
   Traditional Glyph: Spiral

2. YOG-SOTHOTH—All One—Unification—All in One, Vehicle of Chaos, Gate of the Void, Crossing to the Abyss.
   Element: Fire; Zodiac: Leo
   Direction: Immediate South; Time Threshold: Thursday
   Mardukite Pantheon: MARDUK
   Traditional Glyph: Circle

3. NYRALATHOTEP—Crawling Chaos, The Aether "Between"—The Will of the "Old Ones" in "Space" [Outer Space]; Milky Way, the Tortuous Serpent or Path of the Serpent.
   Alias: NyPaLa(t)hotep
   Time Threshold: Wednesday
   Mardukite Pantheon: NABU
   Traditional Glyph: Wand of Power

---

22 *Daath*—the "Gate to the Outside" or Gate of GANZIR (Babylonian) as relayed in the Semitic Hebrew Kabbalah.

4. HASTUR—Voice of the "Old Ones."
Element: Air
Zodiac: Aquarius
Direction: East Time Threshold: Saturday (?)
Mardukite Pantheon: NINIB ADAR
Traditional Glyph: Crescent

5. CTULU—Lord of "Deep Ones," Dreams, the Crossings
of the Abyss.
Element: Water
Zodiac: Scorpio
Alias: Kutulu, Cthulu Direction: West
Time Threshold: Tuesday
Mardukite Pantheon: NERGAL
Traditional Glyph: Trapezoid

6. SHUB-NIGGURATH—The Black Goat, the Black Goat of the
Woods (with 1000 Young), Gate of the North Wind.
Element: Earth
Zodiac: Taurus
Time Threshold: Friday
Mardukite Pantheon: ENKI (some list as ASTOR)[23]
Traditional Glyph: Triangle

◊ ◊ ◊   ◊ ◊ ◊   ◊ ◊ ◊

Make your invocation to MARDUK and SARPANIT. Then call in
(invoke) the Supernal Trinity—ANU, ENLIL and ENKI followed by
a conjuration of the Fires and the Four Beacons ["lamps"] of the
Watchtowers (cardinal directions). Perform the Incantation of
ERIDU and call forth the presence of the personal Guardi-
an-Spirit Watcher. Name the Talisman or Stone (whispering the
name of the Seal or spirit called) and conduct the appropriate
Invocation of the Gate.

---

23 ASTOR—*Astor, Ashtor* and *Ashtoreth* are later Caananite and Hebrew
interpretations of ISHTAR (INANNA).

SYSTEMOLOGY
The Pathway to Self-Honesty

Take control of your destiny and chart your

first steps toward spiritual evolution...

CRYSTAL CLEAR
Self-Actualization Manual & Guide to Total Awareness
by Joshua Free

Realize new potentials of the Human Condition with
the first effective manual of systematic *"Self-Processing."*

Discover amazing power behind the applied spiritual technology
used for counseling and advisement in Mardukite Zuism!

Premiere Edition Hardcover and Paperback Available

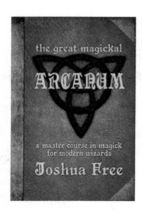

DRACONOMICON
The Book of Ancient Dragon Magick
25th Anniversary Collector's Edition
by Joshua Free

THE DRUID'S HANDBOOK
Ancient Magick for a New Age
20th Anniversary Collector's Edition
by Joshua Free

**ELVENOMICON -or-
SECRET TRADITIONS OF
ELVES AND FAERIES**
The Book of Elven Magick
& Druid Lore
15th Anniversary Collector's Edition
by Joshua Free

JOSHUA FREE
publishing imprint

mardukite.com

Printed in the USA
CPSIA information can be obtained
at www.ICGtesting.com
LVHW040421300124
770335LV00002B/11